start
making
jewellery

start making jewellery

MAKE YOUR OWN BEAUTIFUL JEWELLERY

NICOLA HURST

APPLE

A QUARTO BOOK

First published in the UK in 2008 by
Apple Press
7 Greenland Street
London NW1 0ND
United Kingdom
www.apple-press.com

Copyright © 2008 by Quarto Publishing plc

ISBN: 978-1-84543-221-8

QUAR.JMB

Conceived, designed and produced by
Quarto Publishing plc
The Old Brewery
6 Blundell Street
London N7 9BH

Project editor: **Lindsay Kaubi**
Copy editors: **Bridget Jones, Sally Maceachern**
Art director: **Caroline Guest**
Art editor: **Julie Joubinaux**
Designer: **Graham Saville**
Photographer: **Martin Norris, Philip Wilkins**
Picture research: **Claudia Tate**

Creative director: **Moira Clinch**
Publisher: **Paul Carslake**

Color separation by PICA Digital, Singapore
Printed in China by 1010 Printing International Ltd

10 9 8 7 6 5 4 3 2 1

CONTENTS

Author's foreword	6
About this book	8
Health and safety	9
CHAPTER 1: Getting started	10
Tools and Materials	12
Making a space to work in	18
CHAPTER 2: Techniques and projects	20
Technique 1: Inspiration and design	22
Technique 2: Planning a design	26
Technique 3: Piercing	30
Technique 4: Drilling	34
Technique 5: Filing	36
Technique 6: Soldering	38
Technique 7: Finishing and polishing	42
Project 1: Simple pendant	46
Technique 8: Annealing	48
Technique 9: Using wire	50
Project 2: Simple chain necklace	52
Project 3: Simple silver ring	54

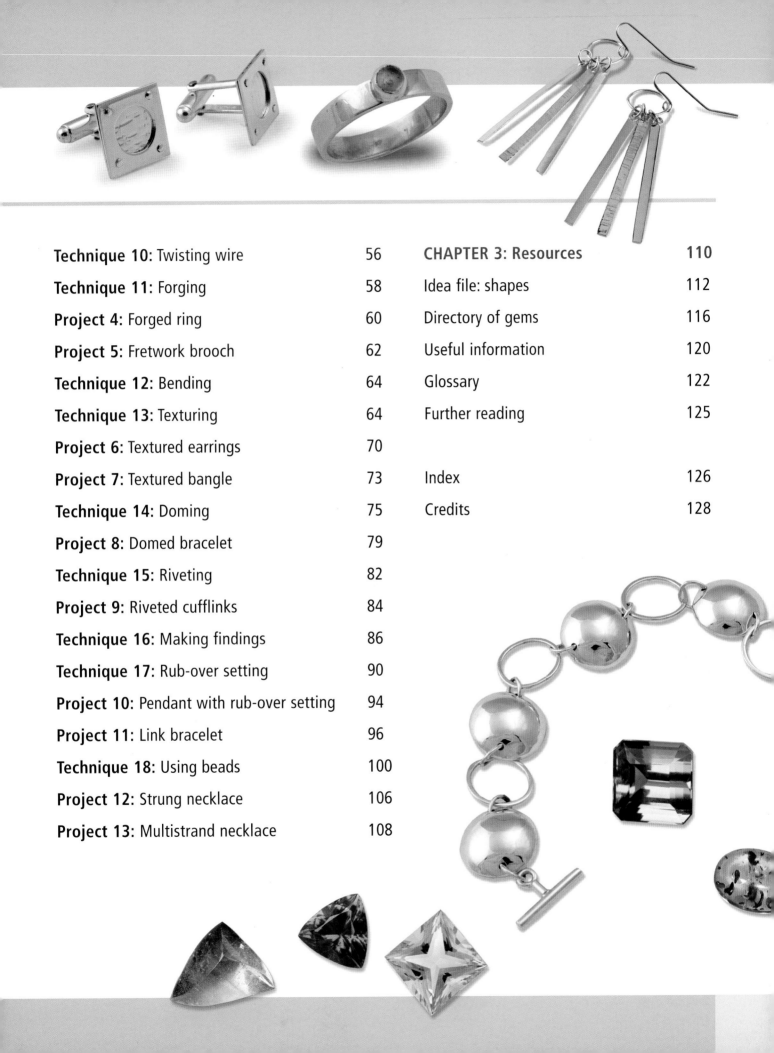

Technique 10: Twisting wire   56

Technique 11: Forging   58

Project 4: Forged ring   60

Project 5: Fretwork brooch   62

Technique 12: Bending   64

Technique 13: Texturing   64

Project 6: Textured earrings   70

Project 7: Textured bangle   73

Technique 14: Doming   75

Project 8: Domed bracelet   79

Technique 15: Riveting   82

Project 9: Riveted cufflinks   84

Technique 16: Making findings   86

Technique 17: Rub-over setting   90

Project 10: Pendant with rub-over setting   94

Project 11: Link bracelet   96

Technique 18: Using beads   100

Project 12: Strung necklace   106

Project 13: Multistrand necklace   108

CHAPTER 3: Resources   110

Idea file: shapes   112

Directory of gems   116

Useful information   120

Glossary   122

Further reading   125

Index   126

Credits   128

AUTHOR'S FOREWORD

My passion for making things and using metal started in my teens, when I began taking apart televisions and using the parts to make jewellery. Then, at college, during my art and design foundation course, I learned how to weld, and that's where my love for metalwork really began. From large steel sculptures I downscaled to jewellery making; so much more manageable and portable. Although I experimented with woods and Perspex, silks and beads, I eventually settled on using metals, predominantly silver and gold.

Jewellery means something different to everyone; it can be very personal. Making a wedding ring, for example, which will be blessed and worn for many, many years has huge meaning, yet the design of the wedding ring is very simple. To be able to make a piece of jewellery that a person can wear comfortably, and with ease, as well as being stylish and elegant, is my priority when I design and make jewellery. This is reflected in the simple and elegant projects in this book.

Teaching jewellery making to beginners and to those who are more experienced has taught me that explaining the techniques in a way that is easy to understand and easy to follow is really important. While working with other jewellers over the years, I have realized that there are several ways to carry out every technique. Each jeweller has their own way of working; their favourite tools; most comfortable way to hold a blow-torch, etc. As you learn the techniques of jewellery making you will find your own way too.

This book shows and teaches the basic techniques for the beginner jeweller as well as showing how to use the techniques in creative projects. First, you will learn about inspiration and planning a design, then you will learn the most basic skills, such as piercing, filing and soldering. Next, you will move onto cleaning up and polishing, as well as other exciting techniques such as texturing and riveting. Once these techniques are mastered you will have the fundamental knowledge and skills to make any piece of metal jewellery. The projects, which are interspersed between the techniques, are easy to follow step-by-step pieces based on the skills learned, which get more challenging as the book progresses. There are handy tips throughout the book and clear pictures of each step. As well as the techniques and projects, you will find guides to which tools to use and setting up a workshop, as well as information on metals, melting temperatures, gemstones and ideas for shapes.

By the end of the book you will have made several pieces of jewellery, from a simple silver ring and easy bangle to a pendant with a rub-over setting. You will have attained the skills you need to be able to make jewellery that you will design and wear with pride.

Nicola Hurst

ABOUT THIS BOOK

This book is arranged into a series of techniques and creative projects that become progressively more challenging as you work through them.

CHAPTER 1: GETTING STARTED

Here you'll find a guide to tools and materials as well as advice on setting up a basic workshop in your own home.

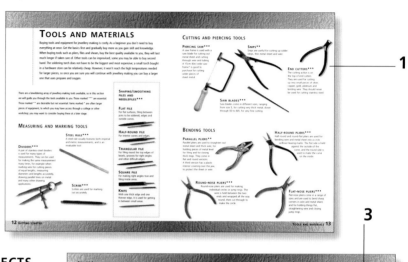

1

3

CHAPTER 2: TECHNIQUES AND PROJECTS

In this chapter are all the essential techniques you need to get started as well as creative practice projects designed to utilise the techniques as you learn them. All techniques are explained in clear steps and handy tips are given along the way.

2

4

5

6

CHAPTER 3: RESOURCES

From ideas for jewellery shapes and a guide to gemstones, to metal melting points and a glossary of terms, this chapter is full of handy information.

1. TOOLS
Photographs and descriptions of tools and equipment help you to identify the key pieces you'll need to start making jewellery.

2. LARGE STEP PHOTOGRAPHS
Each step is shown in large, clear photographs so you can follow the technique sequence.

3. ENLARGED DETAILS
Enlarged details of the making process are shown where necessary so you can see exactly what is going on.

4. TIPS
Jeweller's tips describe shortcuts or ways to avoid mistakes.

5. INSPIRATIONAL EXAMPLES
Occasionally, professional examples are shown that use the featured technique, to show what is possible and to provide ideas for your own designs.

6. MATERIALS NEEDED
Quantities of materials needed and the tools necessary for each project are listed, so you can assemble everything you need before you start.

HEALTH AND SAFETY

Jewellery making is a surprisingly dusty and dirty occupation, and the use of bottled gases, flammable liquids and caustic solutions means you should exercise caution if you intend to work in a home environment. Jewellery making is not in itself a dangerous business or hobby, but careless use of the equipment and materials could lead to accidents. Always make sure you have a first-aid kit ready in case of minor cuts and burns, and having a small fire extinguisher close by would also be prudent.

FOLLOW THESE SENSIBLE PRECAUTIONS TO AVOID ACCIDENTS:

• Always work in well-ventilated, well-lit conditions.

• To prevent leaks, turn off your gas torch at the bottle when you have finished using it.

• Never store chemicals or flammable liquids in unmarked containers. Always keep them out of the reach of children, and preferably in a metal container in the coolest part of the room.

• Keep children and animals away from the workshop.

• Tie long hair back and avoid wearing loose clothing that can easily become caught on equipment.

• Always follow manufacturers' directions when using chemicals, resins and caustic solutions.

• Wear safety glasses when using high-speed polishing equipment and drills.

• Wear a dust mask when using polishing equipment and during any activity that generates dust particles.

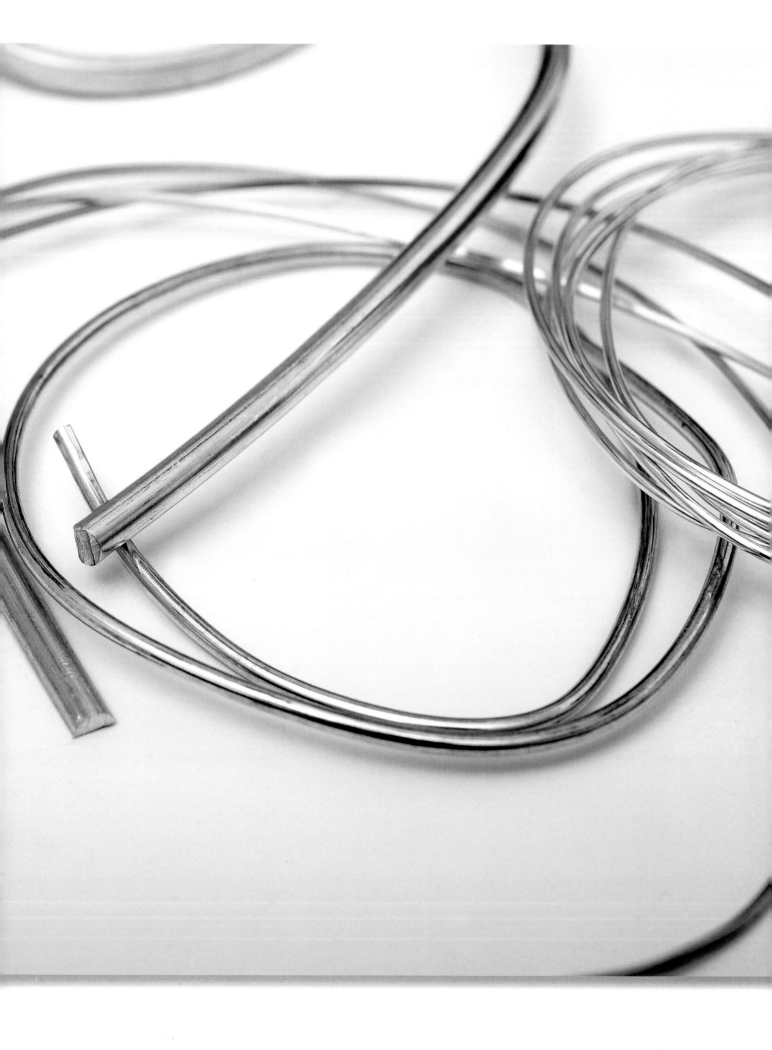

CHAPTER 1:
GETTING STARTED

Every jeweller needs tools and equipment, a space to work in and materials to create the jewellery from. This chapter will help you understand which tools are necessary to start making jewellery and which others you will need as you progress. Materials vary depending on the designs you are making. Try to buy what you need as you need it for each piece. The importance of work space is discussed, an area that is comfortable, clean and safe. In this chapter you will also find advice on getting inspiration, designing and planning and making your ideas a reality.

TOOLS AND MATERIALS

Buying tools and equipment for jewellery making is costly. As a beginner you don't need to buy everything at once. Get the basics first and gradually buy more as you gain skill and knowledge. When buying tools such as pliers, files and shears, buy the best quality available to you, they will last much longer if taken care of. Other tools can be improvised, some you may be able to buy second hand. The soldering torch does not have to be the biggest and most expensive; a small torch bought in a hardware store can be relatively cheap. However, it won't reach the high temperatures needed for larger pieces, so once you are sure you will continue with jewellery making you can buy a larger one that uses propane and oxygen.

There are a bewildering array of jewellery-making tools available, so in this section we will guide you through the tools available to you. Those marked *** are essential. Those marked ** are desirable but not essential. Items marked * are often larger pieces of equipment, to which you may have access through a college or other workshop; you may want to consider buying these at a later stage.

MEASURING AND MARKING TOOLS

STEEL RULE***
A steel rule usually features both imperial and metric measurements, and is an invaluable tool.

DIVIDERS***
A pair of stainless-steel dividers is used for many types of measurements. They can be used for making the same measurement many times, for example when marking wire for cutting pieces of equal lengths, measuring diameters and lengths accurately, drawing parallel lines on metal and many other drawing applications.

SCRIBE***
Scribes are used for marking out accurately.

SHAPING/SMOOTHING FILES AND NEEDLEFILES***

FLAT FILE
For flat surfaces, filing between joins to be soldered, edges and outside curves.

HALF-ROUND FILE
For interior curves and edges.

TRIANGULAR FILE
For filing round the top edges of bezels, grooves for right angles and other difficult edges.

SQUARE FILE
For making right angles true and filing inside areas.

KNIFE
With one thick edge and one thinner edge, it is used for getting in between small areas.

CUTTING AND PIERCING TOOLS

PIERCING SAW***
A saw frame is used with a saw blade for cutting out metal sheet and cutting through wire and tubing. A 15cm (6in) wide saw frame* is good to purchase for cutting wider pieces of sheet metal.

SNIPS**
Snips are useful for cutting up solder strips, thin metal sheet and wire.

END CUTTERS***
The cutting action is on the top of end cutters. They are used for cutting up very small pieces of silver, copper, gold, platinum and binding wire. They should never be used for cutting stainless steel.

SAW BLADES***
Saw blades come in different sizes, ranging from size 5, for cutting very thick metal, down through 00 to 8/0, for very fine cutting.

BENDING TOOLS

PARALLEL PLIERS**
Parallel pliers are used to straighten out metal sheet and thick wire, for holding pieces of metal level for filing and for closing thick rings. They come in flat and round versions. A third version has a plastic interior covering over the jaw, to protect the sheet or wire.

HALF-ROUND PLIERS***
Half-round and round-flat pliers are used for bending wire and metal sheet into a circle without leaving marks. The flat side is held against the outside of the curve, and the round side is used to make the curve on the inside.

ROUND-NOSE PLIERS***

Round-nose pliers are used for making individual circles or jump rings. The wire is held between the two ends and wrapped all the way round, then cut through to make the circle.

FLAT-NOSE PLIERS***

Flat-nose pliers come in a range of sizes and are used to bend sharp corners in wire and metal sheet, and for holding things flat, straightening wire and closing jump rings.

HAMMERS

RAWHIDE OR WOODEN MALLET***

A leather rawhide, wooden or plastic mallet is used to hammer metal without leaving a mark. A mallet is usually used to shape metal without stretching it.

BALL-PEIN HAMMER***

A ball-pein hammer has a metal head with one flat end and one rounded end. The round end is used to shape and texture metal and hammer in small spaces. The flat end is used for stretching metal on a mandrel.

PIN HAMMER***

A lightweight pin hammer can be used for all delicate work. It has one flat end, which can be used for riveting and other small jobs, and one wedge-shaped end that can be used for texturing metal.

PLANISHING HAMMER ***

A planishing hammer with its flat, polished faces is used for smoothing out irregular bumps in raised forms.

FLAT STEEL PLATE***

The flat surface of a steel block is useful for flattening sheet and wire, or to support work as it is forged, riveted or textured with punches or hammers.

RAISING HAMMER**

Raising hammers have a long head and a rounded face and are used for various forming and forging techniques.

FORMING TOOLS

RING MANDREL (BANGLE MANDREL)**

A mandrel is a tapered steel or wooden former that is used to shape metal. Mandrels can be round, oval, square, teardrop or hexagonal in cross-section; the one shown here is a round ring mandrel.

DOMING BLOCK AND PUNCHES**

A doming block is a brass or metal cube with different sized half-spheres moulded into each side. It is used to form metal disks into domes. Doming punches are shaped to fit into each different size of half-sphere in the doming block. They can be made of wood or steel, and are placed on top of the metal disk and hit with a hammer or mallet to form the dome.

CLAMPS AND VICES

RING CLAMP**
Wooden handheld clamps with leather pads are used to hold rings safely, without damaging their shanks, for stone setting.

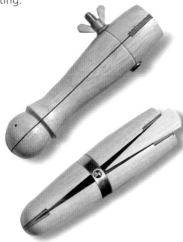

BENCH VICE***
There are two types of bench vice. One is quite small, able to turn in all directions and has 'safe' or plastic jaws. The other is a more heavy-duty vice, which is used to hold stakes, mandrels and draw plates. Ideally both types should be fixed permanently to the bench.

DRILLING TOOLS

ARCHIMEDEAN DRILL AND DRILL BITS (FROM 0.8MM–3MM)***
This is a small, handheld drill that fits into the palm of your hand. Archimedean drills can hold different size chucks, to allow for many different size drill bits, from 0.5mm (76-gauge) up to about 3mm (32-gauge).

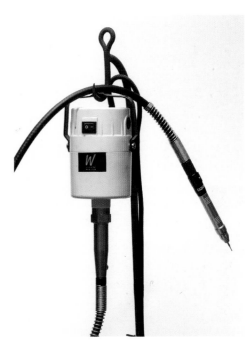

CENTRE PUNCH**
A punch is a small metal tool, similar in shape and size to a pencil. One end has a point and the other is blunt and flat. The point is used to make a mark in the metal where a hole is to be drilled. The blunt end is struck with a hammer.

PENDANT MOTOR**
A pendant motor is attached above the workbench, and has a flexible driveshaft. Anything from small drills, abrasive cutters, grindstones, polishing wheels, felt brushes and muslin mops can be fixed into different sized collets or mandrels, making it a very useful addition to your tool collection.

Soldering equipment

Heat-resistant tweezers***

Tweezers are useful for holding or handling work while annealing, soldering and pickling.

Soldering brick***

You will need a soldering brick or a piece of charcoal on which to solder. You'll also need acid pickle powder and a heatproof glass dish with lid in which to pickle your heated or soldered items.

Solder: easy and hard silver solder***

Solder is found in different grades: hard, medium and easy, which melt at different temperatures so multiple soldering can be done on one item without other joints coming undone.

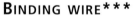

Small brush for applying flux***

Use a dedicated brush to apply flux to your work while soldering. Don't use it for any other purpose.

Binding wire***

Binding wire is useful for soldering jobs that are awkward to balance.

Borax cone and dish***

Borax (flux) is used in conjunction with solder to prevent oxidisation, which blackens metal. The most commonly found and used flux is borax, which comes in the form of a cone that is ground with water in a special dish for the purpose.

Soldering torch***

Perhaps the most important jewellery-making tool is the soldering torch. A large version is used mainly by plumbers, while a smaller-size torch is used by cooks. If you are going to buy one torch, it is best to buy the larger one because this can be used for any of the projects in this book; however, in many cases a small torch from a hardware store will suffice if you're just starting out.

POLISHING EQUIPMENT

EMERY PAPERS AND EMERY BOARDS (GRADES 4/0 AND 1G)***

Emery boards, emery papers and wet-and-dry sandpaper are used for cleaning up after filing. A number that refers to the number of grains to be found in a given area indicates the grade; 150 is coarse, 1200 is fine and used as a polishing paper.

POLISHING COMPOUNDS***

Tripoli and rouge are polishing compounds: essentially greasy compounds containing grit. Tripoli is the coarser of the two compounds and is used before rouge, which gives the fine mirror finish expected of a high polish.

PUSHER AND BURNISHER*

The pusher and burnisher are used for polishing and in the setting of cabochons.

POLISHING MOTOR*

Though not essential, a polishing motor is a very useful item of equipment. Two buffing wheels are available for each grade of polish used.

MATERIALS

In order to complete the projects in this book you will need the following:
- Brass or copper sheet between 0.5mm (24-gauge) and 1mm (18-gauge).
- Silver sheet between 0.5mm (24-gauge) and 1mm (18-gauge).
- Round silver wire: 0.8mm (20-gauge), 1mm (18-gauge) and over.
- Square silver wire 1mm (18-gauge) and over.
- D-shaped wire to make the simple silver ring.

MAKING A SPACE TO WORK IN

Ideally your space should be well lit and ventilated with access to electric sockets and running water. Many people start making jewellery at the kitchen table with a peg clamped in a central position. This is quite adequate, as long as you can sit with your back straight while working. A low chair or stool is preferable so that the peg is just below eye level. However, some tools, equipment and pickles are hazardous, so you may prefer to find another space.

1. Bench   2. Cutout   3. Bench peg   4. Accessible storage

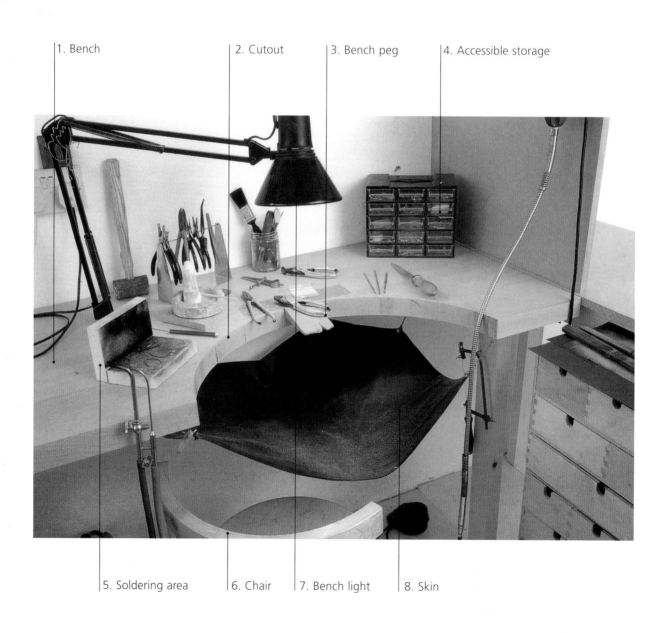

5. Soldering area   6. Chair   7. Bench light   8. Skin

WORKBENCH AND SET-UP

1. If you have a spare corner of a room you can put a small workbench there so that you do not have to put everything away when you stop working. The bench does not have to be expensive; a piece of thick, hard wood with strong legs, about 1m (3 feet) high, is perfect.

2. Traditionally, a jeweller's workbench has a semicircle cut into the top so that the jeweller can sit close to the work and near to all the tools needed.

3. The bench peg is an important tool because most work is done either on the peg or with the support of the peg. It should be attached firmly to the bench with a clamp or screws. Eventually, the peg will wear down and need to be replaced. Cut a 'V' shape in the peg to enable the saw to move easily while piercing. You can cut more Vs and grooves into the peg as needed.

4. The tools that you use most frequently should be readily accessible, either hanging from the bench or in jars – and all an arm's-reach away. Plastic containers with drawers are useful for storing findings, small tools, materials, etc.

5. You will do your soldering on the bench, so protect the area with a piece of metal sheet. You can place the soldering blocks on the sheet.

6. Your chair should be comfortable, allowing you to sit straight at the bench. A chair with wheels is useful.

7. A good bench light is essential. It should shine directly onto your work. You should switch it off while soldering.

8. A skin hanging under the bench catches the falling scrap. You can also use a plastic or metal tray to collect the scrap. Use different pots for different metals.

TIPS

- Work in a well-lit, ventilated space.
- The workbench/table should be 1m (3 feet) high. If it is not, adjust your chair so that your chin is level with the peg.
- The bench should be on sturdy legs and about 30mm (1½in) thick. It should be strong enough to hammer on.
- Make sure the bench peg is securely fitted.
- Use a bench light with a switch to hand, so you can turn it off easily when soldering.
- Have handy drawers on the bench to store small findings, etc.
- If you are working at a table, you can put a tray on your lap to catch filings.

- The floor should be smooth so that it is easy to spot any dropped items.
- It is useful to have a vice attached to the bench. However, if you are using the kitchen table this may not be possible. You may have to put one in the garage or shed instead.
- Try to store your tools in a dry place. You do not want rusty tools. If they do get slightly damp, make sure they are dry before you use them.
- Wear old clothes while at the bench. It is a good idea to wear a thick apron to protect you and your clothes.

INSPIRATION AND DESIGN

Designing a piece of jewellery that is both wearable and aesthetically pleasing can be the hardest part of jewellery making. Design can seem very daunting at first. Start by noticing the jewellery round you. See what other people are wearing and look in magazines and store windows. Note how pieces are made and how they hang or sit. Look at the different materials used, the colours, the sizes and the finish.

IDEAS FILE AND SKETCHBOOK

It can be helpful to keep an ideas file or a sketchbook. Ideas can often come into your head at odd times, like the middle of the night, but try to sketch them down as you think of them, or make a note or two. Cut out magazine pictures and keep them in your sketchbook for future reference. Scraps of material, leaves, etc., can be useful for texture ideas.

If you look round your home you will see shapes, lines, textures and forms that can be transferred into a design for a piece of jewellery. For example, the curve of a pan lid; the way a pipe turns into the radiator; the pattern of a rug or automobile seat cover; the architectural design; or even the house itself.

Many ideas for designs come from nature: leaves, flowers, trees and animals. Other designs derive from the human form: eyes, mouths and fingers.

Experimenting with the techniques in this book will also inspire you. Keep your scrap metal to try out new things, such as reticulation, twisting and doming, and new ideas will form.

IDEAS FILE
Cut out pictures from magazines and keep them in a sketchbook. Or scan and download images and use your computer to help you file them all.

ADAPT IDEAS
Look at photographs of jewellery in books, but try to bring something of your own to any design idea that you find. For example, try simplifying an idea by retaining only the shape or colour of the original piece.

SOLID SHAPES

Solid objects, such as buildings, inspire a design. Find photographs of buildings and use pencil and paper to make tracings. Draw the spaces in between the buildings to see what sort of shapes emerge; record the outline the buildings make against the sky.

NATURAL OBJECTS

Gather a collection of leaves, stones, flowers, shells, and bark and keep them together on or round your workbench. Instead of using the whole leaf or flower for inspiration, try dividing it up and working with just a small section; it could be more interesting than trying to copy it entirely.

WHERE TO LOOK

Museums: Visit museums and study the jewellery, brass- and copperware, agricultural and industrial tools and anything else that you find stimulating. Remember that small local museums can be fascinating and will give you an excellent feel for the topography of an area.

Galleries: Find out where your local galleries are. Visit all their exhibitions and ask to be put on their mailing list – these resources are there for people like you. Recognise which exhibitions you enjoy and those that you don't. It's fine not to like them all!

Exhibitions and open studios: Read local newspapers or listings in magazines for news of other exhibitions. For example, your town may have a festival where local artists open their studios to the public. Take the opportunity to see other artists' work, buy inspirational pieces and talk to them about what they do. Some exhibits and fairs may feature artists actually making their work. Take the opportunity to observe the techniques and tools they use.

Magazines: Most magazines connected with fashion carry jewellery advertisements or even special features about jewellery. Even in magazines that are unrelated to fashion, you may find pictures of people wearing jewellery or lists of galleries exhibiting jewellery. There are specialist magazines too – ask at your local library or news agent to find out what's available.

Books: Books about jewellery provide a fantastic insight into the way jewellers round the world work. Research these sources of inspiration in your local library, or look up jewellery-related books online.

The Internet: Use the image option in a search engine to find inspirational and informative photographs, drawings and graphics related to any subject you can think of from a huge range of sources. As with any source material, don't copy other artists' work, but do use it to inspire you.

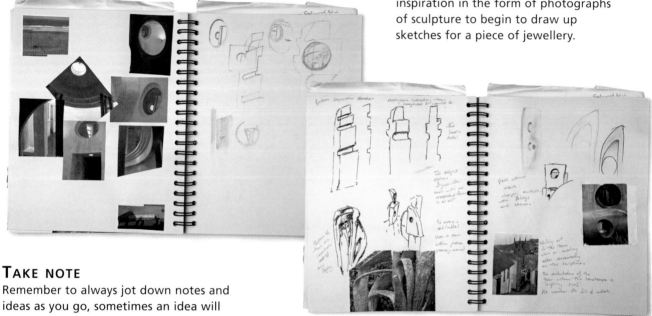

Variety of sources

Here the designer has used source inspiration in the form of photographs of sculpture to begin to draw up sketches for a piece of jewellery.

Take note

Remember to always jot down notes and ideas as you go, sometimes an idea will come to you unexpectedly, or a written note will jog your memory in a way a sketch won't.

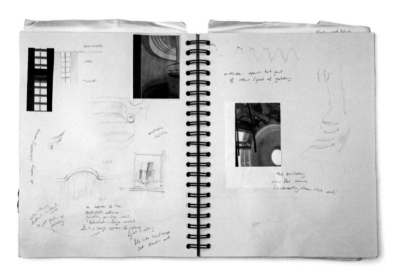

Combining sources of inspiration

By keeping your ideas and sketches together you can pick a line from one, a texture from another, and a form of another and put them together in some way. Sketching them will help you decide what looks good aesthetically and what could become a piece of jewellery. The next stage is to draw the proposed piece to scale (see pages 24–27).

Tips

- Keep a sketchbook with you.
- Be aware of your environment and of other jewellery.
- Visit museums and galleries to look at both contemporary and antique jewellery.
- When you do see jewellery, examine it closely to try and see how it was made; a technique itself can be an inspiration.
- Cut out images from magazines that appeal to you and stick them in your book.
- Think about the scale of the piece. What will it be? A brooch can be much bigger than an earring.
- Decide if you want to use texture.
- Is colour important? If so, think about metal colour or stones. Mixing metal colours can be interesting. Using settings makes the piece more three-dimensional.

INSPIRATION EXERCISE

Try the following exercise to discover a method of finding inspiration that is unique to you. There are no hard-and-fast rules. It is a journey of discovery to find the things that have some kind of emotional effect on you: things that appeal to you no matter what the reason; things that you find interesting, beautiful, controversial, dark or exciting; things that can open up ways of seeing everyday objects in a totally different light. Wherever you live, take time out for a walk. Look all round you – up and down. What shapes can you see outlined against the sky? What is level with your shoulder? What sort of ground are you walking on? What is the road layout? Maybe it is a path through the woods; maybe a trip to the shops – wherever you are there will be something of interest to you if you look closely. How does the light throw a shadow? Can you see reflections in glass? How does a raindrop hang on a leaf? Is there interesting ironwork as you walk through the park? Even if you can't use any of the things you observe directly, just being aware of their influence will have an effect on your ideas.

LOOK ROUND

Inspiration may be found anywhere: a texture seen in the sky or on the surface of a building; the shape of a raindrop; wrought ironwork on a doorway.

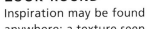

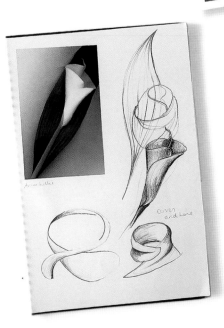

CURVING FORMS

Here, the jeweller used a photograph of a lily for inspiration. The long curves of the flower are translated into a beautiful twist, giving ideas for a ring or maybe a pendant.

PLANNING A DESIGN

If you are a complete beginner it is a good idea to start with very simple designs. Keep a sketchbook to record your ideas, designs and notes (see pages 20–23). Think about what the piece will be – a brooch, earrings, pendant or ring. Now think about the dimensions of the piece and the thickness of the metal.

WORKING DRAWING

You have already thought about scale, texture and colour in the design. It is time to bring it all together to create a working drawing. This will enable you to decide on the actual dimensions of the piece of jewellery, make a mock-up if necessary, transfer the design to metal and make the piece.

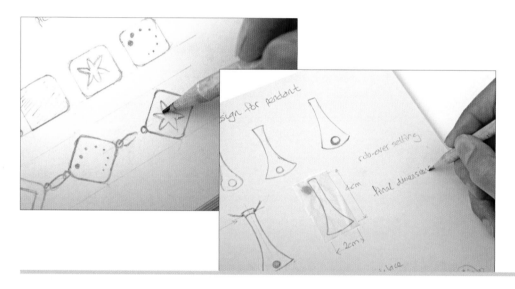

STEP 1 Sketch out the design you want to use and decide what you want the piece to be. Often a design will work as a pendant and earrings so you can make a set. Here, the designs for a bracelet (top) and a pendant (bottom) are shown, several drawings have been used to develop the finished designs.

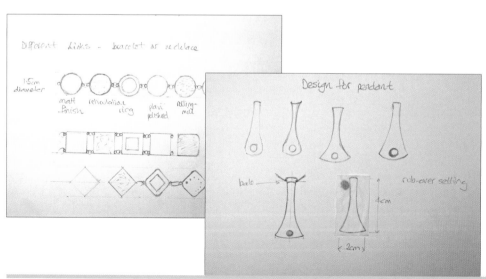

STEP 2 Draw the design to scale and work out the dimensions for the materials needed. If it is a complicated piece with many parts, it can be useful to make a mock-up, but for most pieces an accurate drawing will be sufficient.

TRANSFERRING YOUR DESIGN TO METAL

There are several ways of marking your design onto the metal, depending on the complexity of the design and how accurate you want it to be.

Using a steel rule with a scribe or dividers will give you the most accurate marks on the metal, as long as you measure precisely. You will probably use the steel rule and scribe for marking most designs with straight lines. Use dividers for curves, circles and marking parallel lines. Use a square for precise right angles and other measuring tools for different angles.

If you need to mark a circle, a coin or a small pot can be useful. Draw round it with the scribe. It is a good idea to keep some circular items with different diameters on the workbench.

If your design is more intricate, the easiest way to transfer it to metal is with tracing paper. Trace over the design from your sketchbook with a fine, hard pencil or fine pen. Leaving a little extra space, cut round the design, and glue it onto the metal with a thin layer of paper glue. Make sure the paper is lying completely flat on the metal without any creases or air bubbles.

If there are areas of the design to be drilled and pierced (see pages 30–35), do them first, as there will be more metal to hold onto at this stage. Always saw inside the lines of the section of metal that is to be cut away, to allow for an exact copy of your design. Finish piercing and filing before you remove the tracing paper.

DRAWING THE PATTERN ONTO THE METAL

You can draw your pattern directly onto metal. Use this method if the pattern needs to be very accurate.

STEP 1 Work out on paper the exact pattern needed. This is usually done with a steel rule and a scribe, a pair of dividers or a pair of compasses.

STEP 2 With masking tape, fix down the metal close to your drawing, so that you can take all your measurements easily from the drawing. Start to mark the pattern onto the metal.

STEP 3

The line is now ready to be cut along with the saw. If you use dividers, remember they will scratch the surface. Only scratch in areas to be pierced, because the scratches can be difficult to remove.

FIXING A PATTERN ONTO METAL

Marking out the pattern on tracing paper and then using the saw to cut along the lines of the pattern is a simple and effective way of cutting out. Make sure the tracing paper is stuck down firmly onto the metal, and blow away the dust created as you are sawing.

STEP 1

Trace your finished design onto tracing paper with a fine mechanical pencil. Keep the outline clear, with no sketchy lines.

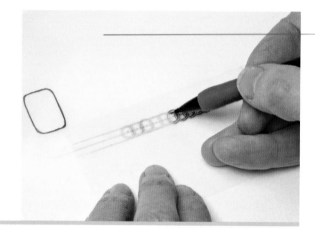

STEP 2

Cut out the tracing paper, leaving a margin round the outside of the pattern.

STEP 3 Remove any protective plastic from the top of the metal sheet.

STEP 4 Use emery paper to remove scratches on the metal surface before cutting. Apply glue to the back of the tracing paper and allow it to air-dry. Place it down onto the metal, making sure that the traced cutting line is not over the edge of the metal. Cut out the pattern with the saw.

HOW TO BUY MATERIALS

You can buy metals in many different shapes and sizes. These include sheets, tubes, rods and wire. Metals are usually supplied by a bullion dealer who will need to know the exact dimensions of the material you are ordering. Most dealers will supply materials by mail order, but it can be useful to go to a store to see all the options that are available.

Sheet metal can usually be supplied in whatever size is needed. Occasionally, with cheaper metals for example, you will only be able to buy a sheet of a fixed size. You should know the width, length and thickness of the sheet metal you need before ordering. For information on the properties of sheet metal see page 120.

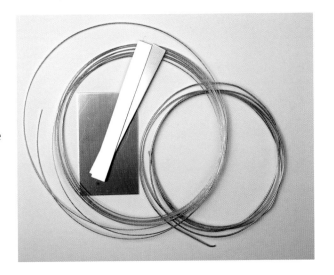

When you buy metals you will pay for the weight. The price of metal fluctuates. Precious metals in particular are subject to price variations according to world markets. This often has a domino effect on the pricing of nonprecious metals as well.

CHAPTER 2
TECHNIQUES AND PROJECTS

The beginner jeweller needs to learn a number of basic techniques, such as piercing, filing, soldering and finishing. This chapter features these techniques and more, interspersed with simple step-by-step projects that show you ways to use them. You can move on to using your own designs when you are confident of knowing how much material to buy.

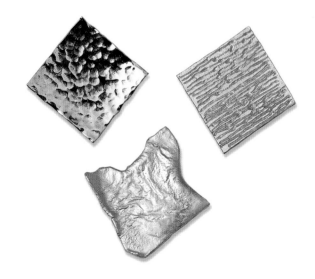

PIERCING

The piercing saw is one of the most useful tools used in jewellery making. The first technique that you should practise while learning to make jewellery is piercing, or sawing, metals. Once mastered, which may take a little practice, the use of the piercing saw will be invaluable, not only for cutting through metal, but also for shaving small areas precisely.

THE PIERCING SAW

To cut through metal, a piercing saw is used with a fine blade. Although various thicknesses of blades can be used, the most useful sizes for a beginner are 2/0 for general sawing and 4/0 for finer work.

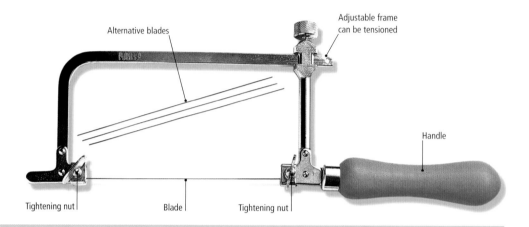

Alternative blades

Adjustable frame can be tensioned

Handle

Tightening nut

Blade

Tightening nut

HOLDING THE SAW

Grip the saw in a relaxed, delicate fashion, but maintain an adequate grip so that the handle does not slip from your grasp.

- Try to hold the saw vertically with the blade against your work. If not vertical, then perpendicular to the surface of the item being cut.

- Work with long, smooth, relaxed strokes, using the full length of the blade and light downwards pressure.

- Cutting only occurs on the down stroke and your sawing action must reflect this, so that the pressure is relaxed on the upstroke and the blade is barely in touch with the work.

- Don't let the blade come out of contact with the work, but maintain a slight 'dragging' contact on the upstroke.

TIP

Sit low at the workbench so that your chin is in line with the jeweller's peg and your back is straight. This way you can easily see the marks on the metal that need to be pierced.

FITTING THE BLADE

STEP 1
Hold the saw and rest it against the jeweller's peg. Carefully take the blade and hold it up to the light. You will see the teeth on the blade, which must face towards you and downwards. Place the top of the blade in the top nut of the saw and tighten.

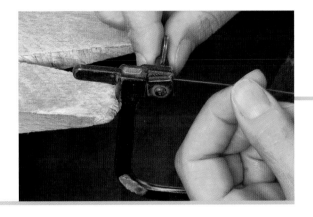

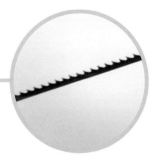

The teeth of the blade should always point downwards if you are holding the blade up.

STEP 2
Hold the handle and push against the peg/workbench, place the other end of the blade in the bottom nut, and tighten. This creates tension in the blade that you will be able to feel.

STARTING TO PIERCE

Mark the cutting line.

STEP 1
Mark the line to be cut clearly on the metal, using a scribe, a metal rule and/or dividers. Holding the saw at a slight angle against the metal edge, move the blade down to create the first cut in the metal.

TIP
Always use the jeweller's peg to hold the metal firmly with your free hand. It doesn't matter if you saw into the peg, that's why it's there.

STEP 2
Straighten the saw so that it is vertical. The blade will cut on the downwards stroke, so a little pressure is needed. Use the length of the blade, slowly and steadily. If the blade is twisted or jarred it will break. At the end of the marked line, undo the bottom nut to free the blade.

PIERCING OUTSIDE CORNERS

First, cut along the first side to a blade's-width past the corner. Then, use tiny up-and-down movements on the spot, without pushing forwards. Use your supporting hand to turn the metal round until the blade is facing in the direction you want to cut, then start to saw forwards again.

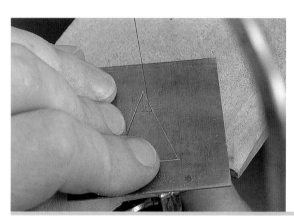

PIERCING INSIDE ANGLES

To saw an acute inside angle, first saw as far as you can into the corner and then back the blade out by moving it up and down. Next, cut across the waste area and then saw into the corner on the other side. This produces a much sharper result than trying to steer round the angle. To make the corner even sharper, tip the blade forwards a little on the last stroke.

PIERCING OUT INTERNAL SHAPES

STEP 1 Before you start to saw, drill a small hole close to, but not on, the line (see pages 34–35).

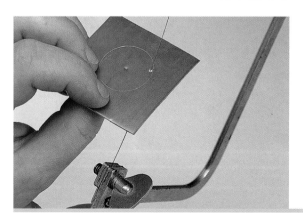

STEP 2 Thread the blade through the drilled hole, having first secured it in the bottom nut of the saw frame. Make sure the marked lines of your design are face up.

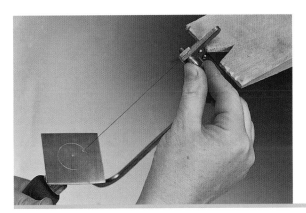

STEP 3
Tip the frame up so the metal slides down towards the handle end of the saw, and then tighten the top nut. Start to saw.

PROFESSIONAL SAMPLES

PIERCED BROOCH
Piercing sheet metal can leave you with delicate, decorative surfaces that are lightweight and practical for jewellery pieces such as brooches, where weight can be a problem.

STONE-SET BROOCH
It takes a steady hand to neatly produce the delicate fretwork in this stone-set brooch. The pattern was achieved by affixing a template to the metal and piercing the shapes marked on it.

SEE ALSO
Drilling, page 34

DRILLING

Drilling is necessary for many jewellery-making techniques: piercing, fretwork, making a hole (or several holes) to allow a saw blade to pass through the sheet metal, riveting and for hanging findings, such as ear hooks or jump rings. Drilled holes can also be used as a decorative feature in their own right.

DRILLS

Most jewellery drills are light and handheld – pendant drill, hobby drill and hand pin drill (also called an Archimedean drill). A fixed pillar drill is very easy to use and ensures that the drill bit moves down vertically.

DRILL BITS

Drill bits vary in size. One of the most useful is a 1mm (61-gauge) drill bit. You will need other sizes for different purposes, such as riveting with 1.5mm (14-gauge) wire, which will require a 1.5mm (53-gauge) drill bit.

TIP

Always wear good eye protection when drilling, as tiny burrs can fly away from the metal.

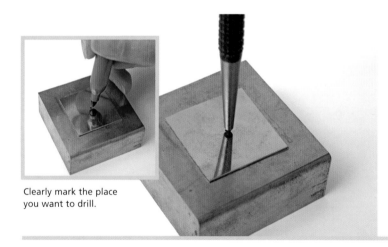

Clearly mark the place you want to drill.

PLANNING AND MARKING

When you plan your piece, decide where the holes need to be drilled and when. First mark the place to be drilled with a scribe. Make the point more visible with a fine marker pen. Place a centre punch over the mark and tap it gently with a hammer. This indentation will prevent the drill bit from skidding over the metal.

Place the correct size drill bit in the chuck.

USING A POWER DRILL

STEP 1 Place the drill bit centrally in the correct size chuck; it should fit without force. Tighten with a chuck key.

STEP 2
Use your fingers, hand or a clamp to hold the metal firmly on a piece of wood so that it cannot move. Carefully position the drill bit on the mark and switch on the power. Use gentle pressure to move the drill down through the metal. If you are using a pendant motor, make sure the drill bit is held perfectly straight, otherwise it will break. With the drill still rotating, remove the drill bit from the metal.

STEP 3
If you need to drill a hole in a small piece of metal it will be very difficult to hold, so drill the hole before piercing the piece out.

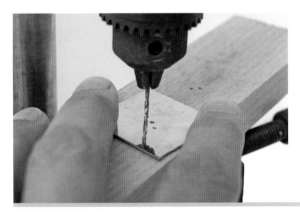

STEP 4
To drill a large hole, first drill a smaller hole and then gradually drill larger and larger until the correct size is achieved.

USING A HAND DRILL
This drill moves at a much slower speed than the power drill, so the hole will also be drilled more slowly. Mark the place to be drilled in the same way as for the power drill. Hold the work firmly and work the drill by raising and lowering the movable nut.

FILING

Filing removes metal in small quantities, to smooth it after piercing or to shape the metal, and files are also used in various techniques, such as bending. Using a file correctly takes some care and practice.

CHOICE OF FILES

Jewellers use hand files of different sizes, grades and shapes, but it is not necessary to buy every type of file at first. Start with the essential types for your projects. The most common file is a grade-2 cut ring, or half-round, but others are also useful, such as flat, round and square files.

So that the filing will be quick and easy, always use the largest file possible for the job and the correct shape to fit the item, for example, use the curved side of a half-round file to file the inside curve of a ring.

Needlefiles are for small pieces or areas that are difficult to reach, not for large areas. The most useful needlefiles are round, three-square, half-round and safety-back.

COMMON FILES

 Flat file
For use on flat surfaces and outside curves. Good general-use file.

 Square file
For use in slots and grooves and for inside angles.

 Triangle or three-square file
For use in tight angles and awkward, small areas.

 Round file
Use on small inside curves and holes.

 Half-round file
Use the curved side for inside curves, and the flat side for general use.

 Knife file
Only use where there is very limited access to corners.

 Crossing or sage-leaf file
Good for filing various inside curves.

 Safety-back file
Good for access to tight corners and angles, because it is only serrated on one side.

BASIC FILING

STEP 1 Hold the metal or piece firmly, resting it against the peg for support. Hold the file flat and level on the piece to avoid accidentally filing away metal (for example along the edge). Move the file away from you in one direction only, keeping it perfectly parallel to the piece to avoid creating unwanted curves at the ends.

STEP 2 Continue filing until the edge is smooth and even. Be firm, controlled and accurate for good results. This can be tedious if there is a large area to be filed away, so practise with the piercing saw to achieve good lines.

TIP

A good way of learning to use a file is to exaggerate the movement by lifting the file away from the piece of work at the end of each stroke. Moving the file in both directions clogs the file and is ineffective. When the edge has been filed a few times, it is easy to see the areas that have been filed and those not yet touched by the file.

FILING A CONVEX CURVE

To file a convex curve, hold the piece firmly against the peg. Use a flat file and long movements round the curve of the piece. Keep turning the piece so that no flat edges are created. Check which areas have been filed and continue until the edge is smooth and even.

SEE ALSO
Piercing, page 30

FILING A CONCAVE CURVE

File a concave curve (such as the inside of a ring) using the curve of a half-round file, or a round file for a smaller curve. Hold the ring, or piece or metal, firmly on the edge of the peg. Hold the curve of the file inside the ring and push the file away from you with some downwards force, at the same time following the curve of the ring, as if you are sweeping round its inside. Keep turning the ring to ensure that the filing is even and smooth. Turn the ring over to file it from both sides.

FILING THE OUTSIDE OF A RING SHANK

Filing the outside of a ring shank takes practice, especially if the ring is convex. Hold the ring firmly against the peg and use a flat file. Follow two curves to avoid developing flat areas. File away from you, round the curve of the ring, turning the angle of the file to allow for the curvature of the shank. For a smooth, even surface, keep turning the ring, sweeping round it as much as possible, without making too many short movements.

USING A NEEDLEFILE

Use needlefiles in very small areas, such as internal piercing or fretwork. It is important to select a file to fit the area. Some places may be so small that a needlefile cannot follow a complete stroke, in which case use shorter strokes. (Sometimes it is easier to use a piercing saw to 'file' these areas, but this takes a lot of skill and practice.)

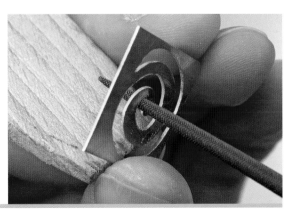

SOLDERING

Soldering is the most common method for joining metal in jewellery making. It is complex and difficult, involves pickling, or cleaning, and can (and does) go wrong. The more you can recognise the stages in heating metal, the faster you will master the technique. Plenty of practice is important for success.

To practise and gain confidence, take each step slowly and observe carefully while heating the metal. Notice how the metal changes colour, and how the solder changes shape before melting and flowing. It is useful to melt a small scrap of silver to see how the metal changes and how quickly it melts.

PREPARING TO SOLDER

Prepare the piece and the soldering area carefully. Switch the bench light off as this allows colour changes in the metal to be seen more easily. Solder will flow only where the metal to be joined is touching, so make sure the seam is perfect and clean, free from dirt and grease.

TIP

If even-sized pieces of metal are used in an item, it is easy to heat them equally with the soldering torch. Soldering often involves different-sized sections, so take care to heat the larger piece first and then spread the heat evenly to create an even temperature. When the solder has run along the whole join, remove the flame at once. Applying a little more heat 'just to make sure' will result in a melted surface.

USING FLUX

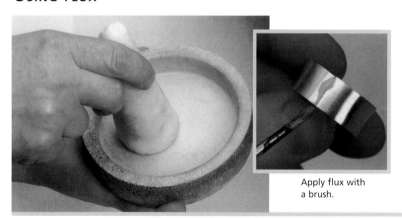

When heated, metal becomes dirty and oxidises, which prevents it from flowing, so it is important to keep the metal clean. Flux helps the solder flow, prevents metal from oxidising, and helps to prevent 'fire stain', which silver develops when heated. Borax is a common flux. It comes as a cone and is mixed to a paste with water in a ceramic dish. Some jewellers use Auflux, which is a liquid, but this can be expensive as it evaporates rapidly.

Apply flux with a brush. A brush is also useful for placing the solder. When the metal is hot the brush will burn, so apply flux and solder when the metal is cool.

Apply flux with a brush.

CUTTING SOLDER

Very small pieces of solder are needed to join metal, and if too much is used the excess has to be filed away, so you will need to cut tiny pieces from the long strips solder is supplied in. First, thin the solder by hammering it (see page 58) or rolling it through a rolling mill (see page 68), which makes it easier to cut. Using snips, cut a fringe into the end of the strip of solder, and cut across the fringe to give small pieces.

SOLDERING

STEP 1 Use a soldering block on the metal plate on the workbench. Place the piece on top and run a flame over it to remove any grease and dust, but not to heat it. Hold a pair of heat-resistant tweezers in your free hand while heating and soldering, ready to move the piece, if necessary, or to replace solder that may move as it heats.

STEP 2 Use a brush to apply flux all over the piece. When flux is heated it tends to bubble before it will settle. Place the solder after the flux has settled to prevent the solder from jumping off the metal.

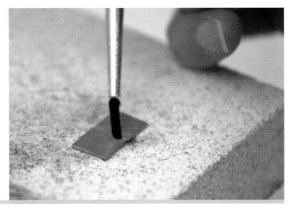

STEP 3 Place a little flux on the brush and use it to place the solder exactly on the join. Use a piece of solder (1mm square [about ½₂in]) about every 1cm (⅜in) – with experience you will learn how much to use and exactly where to put it.

STEP 4 When the solder is exactly in place, heat the whole piece evenly until you see the solder flow along the seam. When this happens, remove the flame immediately and quench the piece in cold water, picking it up with the heat-resistant tweezers.

TYPES OF SOLDER

A piece of jewellery will often need more than one solder join, so solder is available with varying melting temperatures. The most frequently used solders are hard, medium and easy. Hard has a higher melting temperature than medium, which has a higher melting temperature than easy. Enamelling solder is used only for pieces to be enamelled, and extra-easy solder is used mainly for small repairs. To ensure a first solder join on a piece does not come apart when soldering a second join, always start by using hard solder.

SOLDERING A CHAIN

Soldering a chain requires patience as well as practice. Chains have small components
and need to be handled with care using heat-resistant tweezers.

STEP 1 Hold the end of the
chain with the heat-resistant
tweezers, so that the join is at the
top of the jump ring and clearly
visible. Flux the chain well.

TIPS

- Before you start, make sure
  that there are no gaps in the
  jump rings as solder will not
  join a gap. Use two pairs of
  flat-nose pliers to bring the
  ends together, moving
  them sideways.
- Use very small chips of solder.
  This will ensure that there is
  little or no excess for removal
  with a file.
- To make the links oval once
  the chain is soldered, place
  both ends of a pair of round-
  nose pliers in the link and
  carefully open the pliers. This
  will stretch the link into an
  oval. The more the link is
  stretched, the longer it
  will become.

STEP 2 Using the brush,
place a small piece of solder on
the join of the first jump ring held
by the tweezers.

STEP 3 Point the flame
slightly above the join. Sometimes
the force of the flame can blow
such a small piece of solder away.
That will probably be enough heat
to make the solder run. If not,
move the flame down onto the
join. The solder will run very quickly.

The solder will run
very quickly.

STEP 4 Move to the next
jump ring and repeat the process
until all the joins are soldered.
When the whole chain has been
soldered, quench, pickle and rinse
(see opposite).

TEMPERATURE AND COLOUR

Solder will run towards the heat, so an even temperature is important. Judge the temperature of the metal by its colour.

Copper

- When brass or copper is the right temperature for solder to run, it will become a pinkish-red.

- Silver will be pale red when it reaches the right temperature.

Silver

- If silver turns very red, remove the heat because there may be a reason why the solder has not run, such as dirt or oxidisation, or the pieces of metal may have moved apart. Push the metal together with the tweezers, or rinse and pickle the metal, then start again. (Do not use the steel tweezers in the pickle.)

PICKLING

Pickling is the process of cleaning metal after heating to remove flux and oxides. Metal oxidises during heating, producing a residue that has to be removed. The oxidation on silver is called fire stain. If it is not removed completely, it can be seen on the polished piece as a faint grey colour, like a shadow, which is difficult to see until polishing is completed. To prevent this, cover the piece with flux during soldering, then leave it in a pickling solution for a while afterwards. Rinse, file and rub well with emery paper before polishing.

Pickling solutions are acid and they can be dangerous. A common pickle is made with one part sulphuric acid to nine parts water. Alternatively, a pickle powder can be purchased. When making up the solution, always add the pickle powder or acid to water, not water to the powder or acid.

Ideally, the pickle solution should be kept at round 15°C (60°F) to work most efficiently. Speciality pickle tanks can be expensive but an ovenproof glass dish with a lid and a hot plate work equally well.

Always use brass or plastic tweezers when working with pickle because steel in the pickle will cause silver to turn pink. Make sure the piece is rinsed well after being in the pickle solution.

SAFETY POINTS

- If pickling solution comes into contact with skin, wash with cold water immediately. The solution will not severely burn the skin, but it will irritate.

- Wear protective clothing when working. If pickling solution comes into contact with clothing it will not be obvious until the garment is washed, when small holes will appear.

- Always use pickle near running water in case of spills and to rinse metals after pickling.

After soldering the piece, cool or quench it in water by holding it with the heat-resistant tweezers and plunging it into a ready prepared glass container of water. Remove the piece from the water, and then drop it into the pickle but do not let the heat-resistant tweezers touch the pickle solution. Never put hot metal into pickle solution.

FINISHING AND POLISHING

Whether a piece of jewellery has a matt surface or is finished to a shine, it has be cleaned after soldering and pickling. Then it can be finished to the required effect.

SMOOTHING

After excess solder has been removed by filing, taking care not to damage the surface of the metal, emery papers are used to smooth the surface. These come in various grades, from very rough to very fine. Most jewellers use 1G to take away file marks, followed by 4/0 to smooth out the rougher emery paper marks. Wet-and-dry papers are similar to standard emery paper, but less dusty. Shaped emery sticks are used for different tasks or areas.

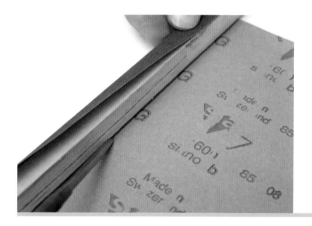

MAKING A FLAT-SIDED EMERY STICK

Take a long stick with 1 cm (⅜in) sides. Lay the emery paper flat on the workbench and place the stick along the edge. Score along the paper using the stick as a ruler, taking care not to cut right through the paper. Then fold the paper round the stick. Repeat the scoring and folding until the whole sheet is wrapped round the stick with tight edges. Secure the paper with masking tape or an elastic band. Tear off paper as it is used.

USING EMERY PAPERS

STEP 1 Work an emery stick, with the higher grade of paper, across the piece in the same way as using a file, to remove file marks. Keep the action smooth and even on the metal, changing direction to avoid making unwanted grooves. A flat-sided emery stick is used on the outside of this ring.

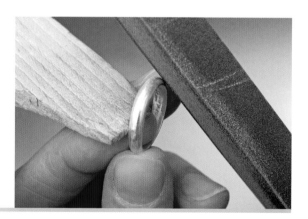

STEP 2 Progress to finer paper to achieve a smooth, even finish on the metal, until it almost looks polished. It is worth spending time with this stage of finishing. Here a round emery stick is used on the inside of the ring.

POLISHING WITH COMPOUNDS

Polishing is usually done with a polishing motor, but you can use a pendant motor for small jobs. Use the same compounds but with smaller mops. You can also use a small hobby drill kit, which is a cheaper option for the beginner.

Tripoli is a dark greasy compound used with calico mops; it takes off the last remaining scratches left by the final emery paper. When polishing the inside of a ring, tripoli is used with a felt mop. Use hot soapy water and an old, soft toothbrush to wash tripoli away before using rouge. Rouge, used with soft lambswool mops, will give a high shine to metal. Take care when using the polisher because the wheels revolve very quickly. Edges of your work can be rounded quickly by mistake, the piece of jewellery can be pulled from your hands and loose items of clothing can be caught in the spindle. Always use two hands to hold the piece of work, and keep moving it from side to side.

USING A POLISHING MOTOR

STEP 1 After switching the polishing motor on, hold the tripoli polishing compound against the calico mop for a few seconds until the wheel has a coating of the compound.

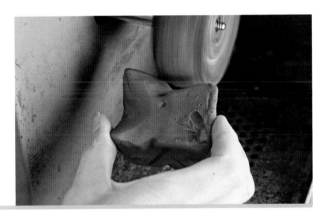

STEP 2 Stand facing the machine. Hold the piece of work just below the central point of the mop. If it is too high or too low it will likely be pulled over or under the wheel. If you feel it being pulled away, let go. Do not let your fingers be pulled with it. Use slight pressure against the mop until you achieve a smooth, even finish. Wash the tripoli off with warm water, grease-removing detergent and a soft, old toothbrush.

STEP 3 This time using rouge and a soft lambswool mop, polish in the same way until you achieve a high shine. Wash the piece again.

POLISHING A CHAIN

STEP 1
Polishing a chain can be difficult and dangerous; if the chain is not held securely it can flick round the mop and pull your fingers. Hold the chain tightly against a flat piece of wood.

STEP 2
Hold the wood so that the chain is vertical against the mop. This prevents the chain from pulling away and being distorted. If you feel the chain (or any other piece) pulling while polishing, let go immediately.

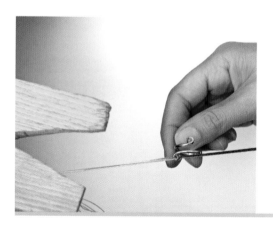

HAND POLISHING

STEP 1
You can use polishing threads to get into very small gaps. Attach a few threads to the bench and rub the rouge bar over them. Now rub the jewellery piece over the threads where needed.

TIP
The compounds are very dirty and the rouge very dusty, so it is very important to wear a dust mask and eye protection while polishing. Wear old clothes and tie back long hair.

STEP 2
You can also use rouge with the suede side of a piece of scrap leather, a polishing cloth or a soft cloth.

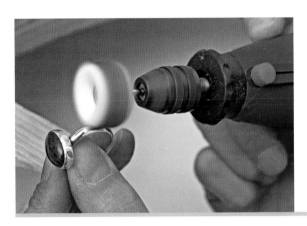

Pendant motor or small hobby drill kit

Although polishing with a pendant motor or small hobby drill kit is much safer than using a polishing motor, you should still wear a mask, goggles and old clothes. Use calico and lambswool mops with tripoli and rouge in the same way as you would for a large polishing motor. Use the bench peg for support.

Small mops

Small mops attached to a pendant motor or a hobby drill are good for getting into awkward places. Use a small felt mop with tripoli for the inside of rings, hold it steady on the piece of jewellery. Take care not to catch the mop on the edges of the metal.

Burnishing

Step 1
Using a burnisher on the edges of a piece can give a wonderful effect, especially if the rest of the piece has a matt finish. Rub the burnisher along the edge until it shines. This will also harden the metal, which is why a burnisher is used to polish earring hooks and stems.

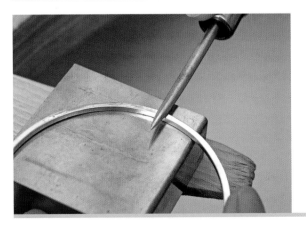

Step 2
A burnisher can also be used to remove a scratch on a flat area. It smoothes the metal outward like planishing.

SEE ALSO
Filing, page 36

SIMPLE PENDANT

It is a good idea to start by using techniques that are already familiar to make a simple piece. This two-part silver pendant features square holes pierced into its surface and contrasting squares of brass soldered onto its components.

TOOLS AND MATERIALS

1mm (18-gauge) silver sheet: 4 x 1cm (1½ x ⅜in)

0.8mm (20-gauge) brass sheet: 1 x 5mm (⅜in x ¼in)

0.8mm (20-gauge) silver wire: 2cm (¾in)

Dividers

Steel rule

Scribe

Piercing saw

Soldering equipment

Centre punch

Drill

1mm (61-gauge) drill bit

Files

Round-nose and flat-nose pliers

Emery papers

Polishing equipment

MARKING THE SILVER

STEP 1 Using dividers or a steel rule and scribe, measure and mark a line 1cm (⅜in) along the silver sheet. Also measure and mark the two square holes to be pierced out. Brass squares will be soldered into the middle of the pendant, so mark the two holes equidistant at either side.

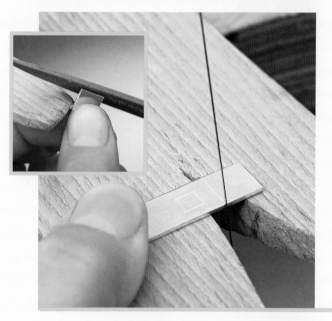

PIERCING AND FILING

STEP 2 Cut the silver using the piercing saw and following the marks. Then file the edges smooth with the flat edge of a file.

STEP 3 Measure, mark, and cut the brass in half exactly, so that you have two 5mm (¼in) squares. File the edges smooth, taking care to keep the two pieces square.

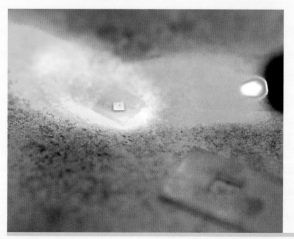

SOLDERING

STEP 4 To solder the brass squares onto the silver, place all of the metal onto the soldering brick. Pass a gentle flame over them and then paint with flux. Cut two small chips of hard solder and place one on each brass square. Heat the brass pieces gently until the solder melts, then turn them upside down, and place them centrally on the two silver components.

STEP 5
Heat one section, passing the flame over the whole piece until the solder runs round the edge of the brass squares. Do not overheat – if the metal becomes red without the solder running, take the flame away, let it cool slightly and start again. The solder will run only if both metals are at the same temperature. Repeat with the other part of the pendant. Quench, pickle and rinse well.

DRILLING
STEP 6
The two parts of the pendant will be joined with a jump ring, and a jump ring will be used to attach the pendant to its chain, so two holes need to be drilled in the top section of the pendant. Using a punch, mark the positions for the holes to be drilled. Drill the holes with a 1mm (61-gauge) drill bit.

FILING AND USING EMERY PAPER
STEP 7
File away any excess solder and then rub both pieces all over with emery paper until they are smooth.

FINISHING
STEP 8
Make two jump rings with the silver wire. Put the rings into the holes, one at the top of the pendant, the other to join the two pieces together. Join the ends of the jump rings with flat-nose pliers and solder using easy solder. Keep the flame away from the rest of the pendant. Pickle the pendant and rinse it well. Then polish it with tripoli and rouge.

SEE ALSO
Piercing, page 30
Drilling, page 34
Filing, page 36
Soldering, page 38
Finishing and polishing, page 42
Making findings, page 86

ANNEALING

When metal is worked in any way by being bent, hammered, filed and so on, it becomes hard and will eventually break if not softened. The technique of annealing is an easy one that is essential to prevent metal from being overworked. Once annealed, a piece of metal will stay soft until worked on again, and it can be annealed as many times as necessary. It is a good idea to anneal a piece of metal before working on it to make bending or shaping easier. Different metals have different melting temperatures and therefore different annealing temperatures.

THE ANNEALING FLAME

The annealing flame is softer than that used for soldering, and is therefore less likely to oxidise the metal. The colour of the metal at annealing temperature is dull red, at which point it is fully softened – any hotter and the structure of the metal could be damaged.

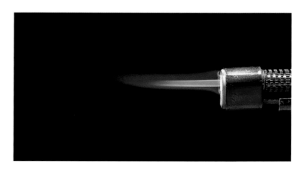

A SOFT FLAME
An annealing flame should be soft so that it heats the metal evenly.

STEP 1 Place the metal on a charcoal block or prop it against a soldering brick to allow the heat to circulate.

STEP 2 Hold the soldering torch in one hand and a pair of heat-resistant tweezers in the other (tweezers in the right hand if you are right handed) and pass the flame gently over the metal. If it is a large sheet, start in the centre and work towards the edges as the piece becomes pink.

STEP 3
Take care not to overheat any one area. Brass or copper should become a red-pink colour.

STEP 4
Silver should become pink and gold should be red-pink. To anneal the metal, keep it at this temperature – no hotter – for about 10 seconds. Quench copper or brass in cold water immediately. Quench silver in cold water after a few seconds. Leave gold to cool rather than quenching.

SILVER
Silver becomes pink when annealed.

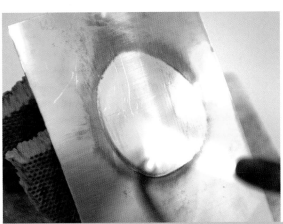

COPPER AND BRASS
Copper and brass become red-pink when annealed.

SEE ALSO
Soldering, page 38

USING WIRE

Different metals are available in many shapes of wire that can be widely used in jewellery making for basic items or more creative forms. From shaping findings such as ear wires, jump rings, hooks and chains using round wire to forming a simple silver ring with D-shaped wire, learning to bend wire is an essential and versatile technique.

BENDING WIRE

To bend wire into a curve, use half-round or round-nose pliers, placing the round part of the pliers on the inside of the bend. Unless the wire is very thin, it will have an element of spring to it. Always anneal wire before shaping, because this allows it to bend more easily and create smoother curves.

Other useful tools include steel rods for making jump rings. In this way larger rings can be made with half-round pliers, or a ring mandrel or bangle mandrel can be used. The principle of the technique is the same no matter what size piece is made or which tool is used.

MAKING A SIMPLE CURVE

STEP 1 Take a reel of relatively thin wire, 1mm (18-gauge) and, at first, just using your hands, notice how soft it is, and how it can be bent using fingers without the need for pliers.

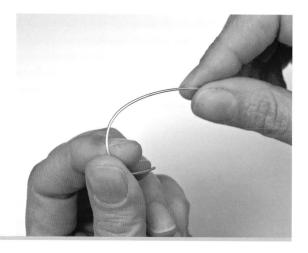

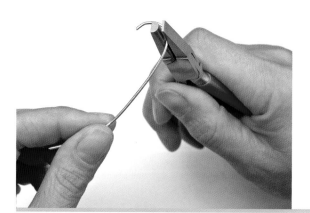

STEP 2 Most items made from wire are precisely bent. Hold the wire with some pliers and bend it round the pliers using your fingers. It is important to use half-round or round-nose pliers, so that they will not cut into the soft metal.

MAKING JUMP RINGS

Use round-nose pliers to make a jump ring by holding the wire at the place along the pliers for the size of jump ring you want. Round-nose pliers taper to a point, so if you want a small jump ring use the tip, if you want a large jump ring use the base. Bend the wire round the pliers with your fingers. Then cut the wire with end cutters or a piercing saw.

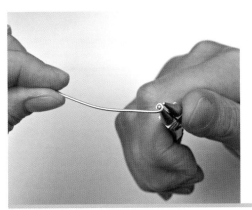

MAKING A WIRE SPIRAL

STEP 1
This is fun and the spiral can be put to several uses, for example as a decorative catch or as detail on a piece of work. Hold the end of a length of wire in round-nose pliers and bend it round using your fingers, keep bending the wire while turning the pliers.

STEP 2
Once the spiral is started, hold it in your fingers, without the pliers, and continue bending the wire round itself.

STEP 3
The finished spiral, with hooked end, looks decorative and is also useful.

WIRE SHAPES

Here are a few examples and ideas for shapes that can be easily achieved through bending wire and how to use them.

Heart shape: Use 1.2mm (16-gauge) wire to make this shape for a pretty pendant.

Fine zigzag: Wire of less than 18-gauge (1mm) was used for these zigzag forms. Solder them on a flat background as decoration on a drop earring.

Chunky zigzag: Use 2mm (12-gauge) wire for this thicker zigzag.

Earwire: Bend a length of 0.8mm (20-gauge) silver wire into this shape for an earring. The long curve fits through the ear and the little ring will hold any small piece that will hang from it.

SEE ALSO
Annealing, page 48
Making findings, page 86

SIMPLE CHAIN NECKLACE

This simple necklace is made with round silver wire, which has been turned into various sizes of jump rings, textured with a planishing hammer and soldered. The chain is large enough to fit over the head and so does not need a clasp. You can use different numbers of links to vary the design. Alternating copper or brass wire with the silver would also add another dimension to the necklace.

TOOLS AND MATERIALS

1.5mm (15-gauge) round silver wire: 2m (6 feet)

Ring mandrel

Piercing saw

Flat-nose pliers

Soldering equipment

Flat steel plate

Planishing hammer

Files

Emery papers

Polishing equipment

STEP 2 Cut through the rings with the piercing saw. There will now be lots of slightly different sized rings.

STEP 3 The rings have to be joined, textured and then cut open again to make the chain. Begin by joining the ends of each ring with flat-nose pliers. Use hard solder to solder them together.

MAKING THE RINGS

STEP 1 Holding one end of the wire tightly at the top of the ring mandrel, turn the wire round the mandrel. Make sure it is pulled tightly and firmly and that each ring is close to the next one. Continue until the whole length has been used.

TEXTURING

STEP 4 Pickle, rinse and dry the rings. Place each one in turn on the flat steel plate and texture with the planishing hammer. The harder the hammer hits the rings, the more they will be distorted and textured.

Linking the rings

Step 5
Use a piercing saw to cut open half the rings on the join, where they were soldered.

Step 6
Use flat-nose pliers to open a ring. Thread it through a soldered ring and close the join. Continue until all the rings have been used and all the joins are closed again.

Step 7
Solder each join again. Hold each ring in turn with the heat-resistant tweezers as you move along the chain, until they are all soldered and secure.

Step 8
Remove any excess solder with a file. Work over the same area with a range of grades of emery papers.

Step 9
Polish with tripoli and rouge. Hold the rings carefully, one by one against the mop. Take care to ensure that the rest of the chain does not get caught in the wheel.

See also
Soldering, page 38
Finishing and polishing, page 42
Using wire, page 50
Texturing, page 66
Making findings, page 86

SIMPLE SILVER RING

Make a simple silver ring using D-shaped silver wire. This is a quick and easy project, ideal for beginners. Once you know how to make a simple ring, you can use this technique time and again, adding texture, other metals and settings or using different wires or sheet metal.

TOOLS AND MATERIALS

6-gauge (4 x 2mm) D-shaped silver wire: 6.5cm (2½in) (length depends on finger size)

Piercing saw

Half-round pliers

Parallel pliers

Soldering equipment

Half-round file

Ring mandrel

Wooden mallet

Emery papers

Polishing equipment

TIP

Silver wire is usually soft enough to bend into a ring shape. But if you're working with thicker wire, or wire that has been worked and become hard, anneal it before the bending process.

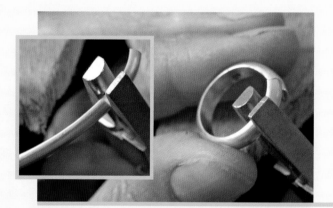

STEP 1 Find the ring size by wrapping a strip of paper round the finger. Mark precisely where the paper overlaps and cut across the line. Measure the strip and add on the depth of the metal, then cut a length of silver wire to this size. Using half-round pliers, bend the silver wire into a rough ring shape.

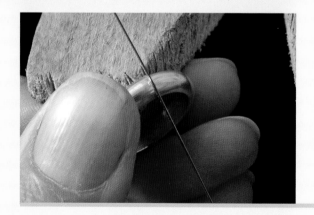

STEP 2 To make the ends fit perfectly against each other, hold the ring tightly together against the peg, and saw through the join. This will shave away any excess that might be preventing a good join. You may have to repeat this process until the two ends fit together precisely. Hold the ring up to the light to check the join.

STEP 3 Use the parallel pliers to move the ends so they overlap each other, and bring them back together. This will create tension in the ring, holding the ends tightly together.

SOLDERING THE RING

STEP 4 To solder the join using hard solder, cover the ring with flux and place solder on the inside of the join. Heat the ring evenly until the solder melts. Turn the ring around and heat from the outside of the join until you can see the solder run through the join. Quench, pickle and rinse.

STEP 5 File away any excess solder, applying even pressure all the way round the join. Put the ring onto the mandrel and use the mallet to knock it into shape. Hammer and turn the mandrel round so the ring is hammered evenly. Turn the ring over on the mandrel, and repeat.

FILING

STEP 6 Hold the ring against the peg. Use the file to file inside (with round side) and outside the ring (with flat side) with a steady, even pressure until the silver is smooth with no fire stain. Use the whole length of the file and turn it in the curve of the ring so no flat areas appear.

STEP 7 Use emery papers in the same way as the file, using a round emery stick for the inside of the ring and a flat stick for the outside. Use various grades of papers until the ring is smooth and ready to be polished. Polish with tripoli and rouge.

SEE ALSO
Filing, page 36
Soldering, page 38
Finishing and polishing, page 42
Annealing, page 48

TWISTING WIRE

Wire twisting is an easy technique that adds depth and interest to a piece of jewellery. Wire can be plaited, knitted, twisted and crocheted. Different metals can be used together for colour, such as silver and brass, or gold; three different colour golds together are frequently used. Combining differently shaped wires together is another way to achieve interesting effects.

Anneal wire before twisting, and anneal it again if it is to be manipulated further. Once wire has been twisted it can be hammered, rolled through a mill, joined onto other parts of a piece or made into a ring.

WIRE SAMPLES
Samples showing a range of twisted, hammered and plaited wires.

Twisted, two round wires

Twisted, two square wires

Twisted, round and square wires

Twisted, two colours, round and square wires

Twisted, three round wires

Plaited, three wires

Rolled

Hammered

SEE ALSO
Drilling, page 34
Soldering, page 38
Finishing and polishing, page 42
Annealing, page 48
Forging, page 58

TWISTING WIRE
STEP 1 Using 1mm (18-gauge) wire, mark every 15cm (6in) and cut the wire to make three pieces.

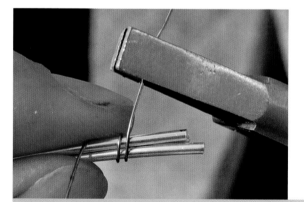

STEP 2 Use binding wire to bind the ends together at one end. Flux well. Place pieces of hard solder into joins and solder the ends together.

Solder the ends together.

STEP 3 Remove binding wire, pickle and rinse. Place the soldered end into a vice, hold the other ends with parallel pliers and twist tightly to create an even twist along the length of the wires.

SOLDERING AND PLANISHING

STEP 1 Lay the twisted wire on the soldering brick and place pieces of solder along the joins every 1.5cm (½in). Gently heat the whole piece until the solder runs along the joins. Pickle and rinse.

Pickle and rinse.

STEP 2 Cut away the uneven ends of the twisted wires using a saw. Place the twisted wire onto a flat steel block or anvil, and, using the planishing hammer, hammer the wire until it is flat at one end. Note that using a planishing hammer results in a smooth, even surface.

The smooth hammered surface.

TO MAKE A PENDANT

If you want to make a pendant from your twisted and hammered wire, make a hole at the flat end and hang it from a fine silver chain.

Mark a hole at the flat hammered end with a scribe. Drill out the hole, then pierce the area to be cut out. File the hole smooth, then file and emery the whole pendant and polish with tripoli and rouge.

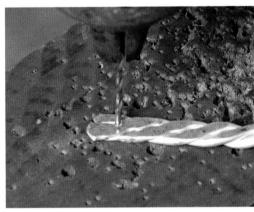

FORGING

Forging is the technique used to force metal to move in any direction with the blow of a hammer. Forging can also be used to texture, flatten or spread metal. Various hammers, steel stakes or flat plates, such as an anvil, are used, and all must be kept to a high polish so as not to transfer unwanted marks to the metal.

THE SOUND OF FORGING

Before it is forged the piece must be annealed. After forging for some time, the hammer will make a different sound when it hits the metal, it will ring, and the metal will seem springier against the anvil or steel plate – this is a sign that the metal is becoming brittle and it must be annealed again.

CURVING METAL

STEP 1 To curve a piece of metal, use a raising hammer and an anvil or flat plate. Hammer along one side of the metal using only one side of the hammer.

STEP 2 Hammering along one side only will elongate the metal on that side and push the metal on the other side into a curve.

TIP
Use a piece of metal that is larger than required for the piece, because it is easier to remove unwanted metal at the end rather than add metal. It is also easier to hold a larger piece without hammering your fingers!

FLATTENING AND BROADENING METAL

To flatten and broaden an area of metal, use a flat-headed hammer, for example the flat end of a planishing hammer. Hold the metal flat on the anvil or flat plate, and apply straight, heavy strokes of the hammer.

LENGTHENING METAL

To lengthen a piece of metal use the raising hammer at right angles to the strip of metal to ensure that the hammer blows fall straight down onto it.

TIP

Experiment with different hammers to discover the different ways in which they displace the metal. A curved hammer creates an angle in the metal. The same applies to the steel plate on which the metal is hammered.

USING A FLAT PLATE

Using a flat plate will give a totally different effect than that achieved by using a rounded, domed end of a doming block, or the curve of a mandrel. 1 shows round wire before forging. 2 shows round wire once the forging process has begun. The three pendants (3, 4 and 5) were all forged using the same technique but each is subtly different and unique.

1   2   3   4   5

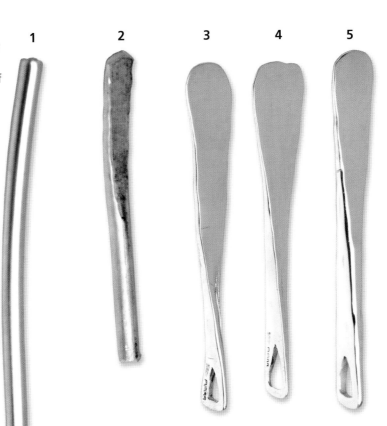

SEE ALSO
Annealing, page 48

FORGED RING

This silver ring is made from one piece of wire, forged into different shapes at each end and in the centre, which becomes the bottom of the shank. As it is hammered, and therefore hardened, there is no need to join by soldering. This makes the ring flexible in size.

TOOLS AND MATERIALS

2mm (12-gauge) round silver wire: 8cm (3in)

Soldering torch

Flat steel plate

Planishing hammer

Ring mandrel

Wooden mallet

Round-nose pliers

Files

Emery papers

Polishing equipment, including polishing threads

PREPARING THE WIRE

STEP 1 Start by annealing the silver wire. Pickle, rinse and dry well. Place the wire on the steel plate. Use the planishing hammer to hit straight down on the central area of the wire, spreading it out and making it wider.

STEP 2 Turning the wire, forge each end in the same way as the centre, so that they widen at the ends and gradually taper in.

MAKING THE RING

STEP 3 Use the hammer to even the wire between the ends and the centre. At this point you'll need to anneal again as the wire will be hardened and it needs to be shaped round the ring mandrel.

STEP 4
Use your fingers to bend the wire round the ring mandrel. You may need to use the wooden mallet to knock the ends completely round. The ends will overlap each other.

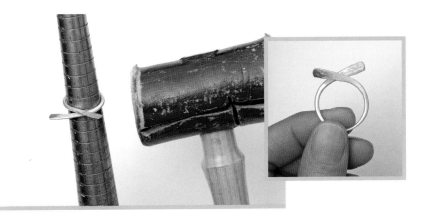

STEP 5
Once the ring is the correct size and shape, take a pair of round-nose pliers and bend each end into a small spiral that faces out from the ring.

FINISHING

STEP 6
File any sharp areas smooth, but do not change the shape of the ring too much. Try not to lose the texture created by the planishing hammer. The underside of the spirals may need smoothing slightly with a half-round file. Emery where needed and polish. The insides of the spirals may need to be polished with polishing threads.

SEE ALSO
Finishing and polishing, page 42
Annealing, page 48
Using wire, page 50
Forging, page 58

FRETWORK BROOCH

Piercing, also known as fretwork, is the term used by jewellers for cutting metal with a piercing saw. This technique can be used to create ornamental patterns in the metal to give a delicate finish to a piece of work.

TOOLS AND MATERIALS

1mm (18-gauge) silver sheet: 5 x 2.5cm (2 x 1in)

0.8mm (20-gauge) silver wire: length required for pin, see Step 6

Centre punch

Drill

Piercing saw

Files

Soldering equipment

Silver brooch fittings

Emery papers

Polishing equipment

Pin hammer

Round-nose pliers

Steel burr

Flat steel plate

Rivet (see page 82)

STEP 1
Copy the design using tracing paper and cut it out, leaving a little paper round the design. Attach the paper to the silver using double-sided tape, making sure the whole piece of paper is stuck firmly to the sheet. Use a pencil to mark the points where the holes should be drilled for the fretwork, then punch each mark. Drill the holes.

PIERCING
STEP 2
Undo one end of the saw blade and place the blade through the first drilled hole and tighten the blade in the saw frame. Saw on the inside of the drawn line to pierce the shape until it falls out. Repeat with the remaining shapes. When the shapes are removed, cut round the outline of the piece. Remove the paper and tape from the silver.

STEP 3
Find the correct size needlefile to fit the pierced shapes and file the edges until they are smooth and even. File round the edge of the brooch using a larger file, such as the flat side of a half-round file.

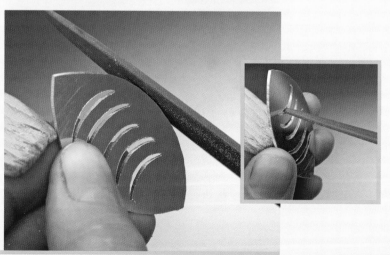

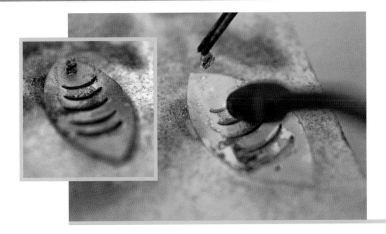

SOLDERING THE FITTINGS

STEP 4
Prepare and flux the piece as usual. Melt a small chip of easy solder onto the bottom of each brooch fitting. Gently heat the brooch until it is nearly pink. When you can see that the metal is pink, without taking the flame away, place the fitting on the silver using heat-resistant tweezers and the solder should run immediately. If the solder does not run, remove the fitting and repeat the process. Remove the heat as soon as the solder has run – if you leave the small brooch fittings in the flame they will melt. Pickle and rinse the piece.

STEP 5
Attach the second fitting to the brooch, as in Step 4. Then use emery papers to smooth the brooch front and back, and polish it.

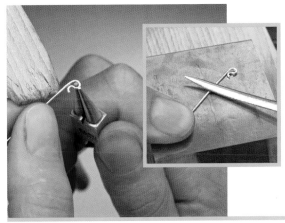

MAKING AND ATTACHING A PIN

STEP 6
Cut 0.8mm (20-gauge) silver wire to the length required for the pin (measure the space between the brooch fittings) and file one end to a point. Use round-nose pliers to bend the other end into a hook. Harden the pin using a steel burr and a steel plate.

STEP 7
The final step to complete the brooch is to rivet the pin onto the fitting. Place the pin in position in the fittings, making sure the hook or hole in the pin is aligned in the fitting. Fix a small rivet through the fitting and pin.

STEP 8
Place the brooch on the flat plate and gently tap the rivet with a pin hammer until it is splayed at each end, is secure and will not fall out.

SEE ALSO
Piercing, page 30
Drilling, page 34
Soldering, page 38
Finishing and polishing, page 42
Using wire, page 50
Riveting, page 82

BENDING

Metal wire and sheets can be bent in various ways using fingers, pliers, mandrels, the vice or stakes. Fingers are the least damaging to metal, so are always preferable, but they cannot achieve a precise bend and are not always strong enough. The tools depend on the size and weight of metal and the piece – holding metal firmly in pliers and bending it round them by hand is a practical method, and practice will help to perfect bending techniques.

BENDING WIRE

PREPARATION FOR BENDING

Carefully choose the correct pliers for the task to avoid making unwanted marks in the metal. Wires and sheets will probably need to be annealed before bending, but they will be softer and easier to mark.

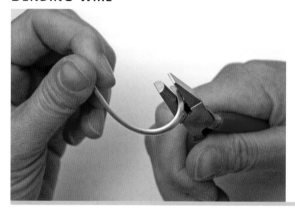

STEP 1 To bend wire into a circle or ring shape, hold the end of the wire with a pair of half-round pliers, with the rounded nose inside the ring.

STEP 2 Carefully bend the wire round with your fingers, moving the pliers along the wire until you have the required shape.

BENDING WITH A RING MANDREL

Rings can also be shaped using a ring mandrel. Bend the wire round the mandrel with your fingers, then gently tap it with a mallet.

BENDING A RIGHT ANGLE

STEP 1
To bend wire or a sheet at a sharp angle, making straight sides, first mark the line where the metal is to be bent with a scribe and a rule.

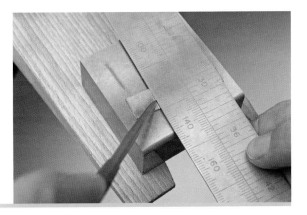

BENDING LARGER PIECES
Use larger mandrels and stakes to bend larger pieces, for example for bangles. Sheet metal can also be bent in this way.

STEP 2
Use a three- or four-square file to file a groove into the metal.

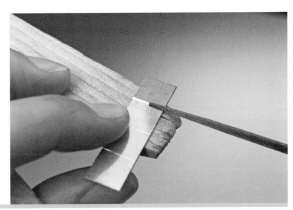

STEP 3
Bend the metal into a perfect, straight angle using parallel pliers, or by placing it in the vice for larger pieces. Take care to protect the metal from the rough teeth in the vice.

STEP 4
Solder the groove to strengthen the bend in the metal.

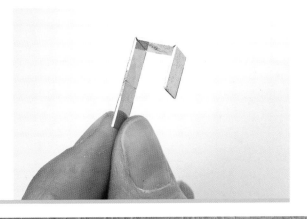

SEE ALSO
Annealing, page 48
Using wire, page 50

TEXTURING

Texturing adds another dimension to the design and finish of jewellery. There are so many ways of bringing texture to metal that it is a good idea to experiment with brass or copper to find the techniques and finishes that you prefer, and then to perfect them before working in more expensive metals, or on specific pieces.

DIFFERENT METHODS

Metal can be textured by hammering, fusing, melting, rolling patterns using a rolling mill, engraving, inlaying and by using different mops with a polishing machine or pendant motor. Some of these techniques are more advanced or may require equipment beyond the scope of the beginner. Here are a few textures that can be achieved easily with basic tools, using simple techniques.

SAFETY POINTS
• Wear safety goggles when using a mop or brush, because fine pieces of metal will fly round.

TEXTURING WITH HAMMERS

STEP 1
Different hammers can be used to create various marks and textures on metal. A tiny pin hammer will make distinct marks.

STEP 2
A heavy ball hammer will create a completely different texture.

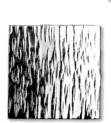

Depending on the hammer used, different textures can be achieved: above: ball-end hammer; left: pin hammer.

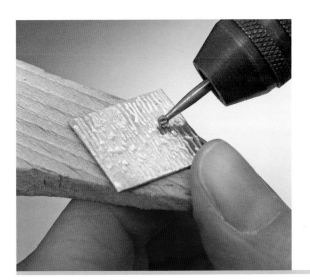

USING A PENDANT MOTOR

Textures can be made using a pendant motor with various attachments. A small burr will grind indents into the surface of the metal. These can be as shallow or deep as required, depending on the pressure applied.

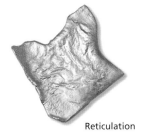

Use a pendant motor to make marks of varying depths.

TEXTURING SMALL AREAS

To apply a matt finish to a small part of a piece, mask off the surrounding area with masking tape. Finish the piece with emery paper, as usual, and polish with tripoli, then use a fine wire brush to create a matt finish. The same finish can also be achieved using a brass brush, with detergent and water. Use the detergent to prevent brass deposits from forming on the metal.

RETICULATION

A random texture can be achieved by fusing, or reticulation, a technique that melts the surface of the metal, but not the whole piece. Heat the metal without using flux until the surface becomes shiny and starts to shimmer, then remove the heat immediately, before the metal melts completely. Not using flux allows the oxides to form and hold the surface intact.

Reticulation causes a random surface texture.

Using a rolling mill

Using a rolling mill is probably one of the best ways to texture metal because many different textures can be created with the one tool. However, a rolling mill is expensive and not usually beginner's equipment. There may be one at your local college or art school. Patterns can be imprinted onto metal by passing it through the rolling mill with, for example, paper, leaves, wires and fabrics.

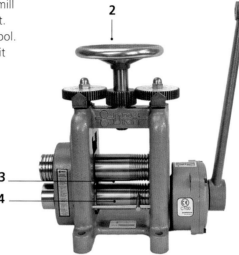

A rolling mill

1. Handle.
2. 'T' handle used to adjust gap between rollers.
3. Feed metal 'sandwich' in here (gap can be adjusted).
4. Polished hardened steel rollers.

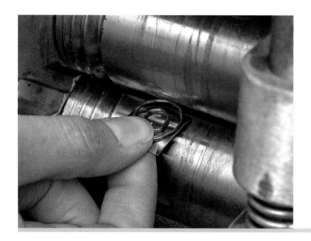

Step 1

Anneal and clean the metal to be textured and adjust the two rollers so that they leave a gap the same thickness as the metal that you're using. Feed the metal and item you're texturing it with in between the rollers and turn the handle.

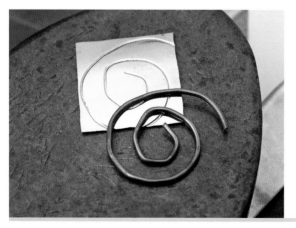

Step 2 In this case a
metal spiral has been used but you can try various materials with different metals to discover new patterns (see opposite).

This is just one example of the many ways texture can be created using a rolling mill.

ROLLING MILL TEXTURES

Here are just a few examples of the type of textures and patterns that you can achieve with this technique. As you can see, the process can be used for very subtle surface finishes as well as bold imprints.

Impression made using high-rag content, heavy watercolour paper.

Impression made using coiled and curved pieces of steel binding wire.

Impression made using Japanese paper.

Impression made using lace from an old curtain.

Impression made using string.

Impression made using a pattern cut out of watercolour paper.

Impression made using a combination of different textures: a dried leaf, cut paper and plaiting.

Impression made using a feather.

SEE ALSO
Finishing and polishing, page 42
Annealing, page 48

TEXTURED EARRINGS

There are many ways of introducing texture to metal. This pair of earrings shows how to create different textures and how they can be used together to create a unique effect.

TOOLS AND MATERIALS

0.6mm (22-gauge) silver sheet: 2.7 x 4cm (1⅛ x 1½in)

0.8mm (20-gauge) silver wire: 30cm (12in)

Steel rule

Dividers

Piercing saw

Files

Emery papers

Pin hammer

Flat steel (plate)

Steel rod

Soldering equipment

Flat-nose and round-nose pliers

Brush mop (a mop that gives a matt finish)

Polishing equipment

TIP

Two of the silver strips will have a matt finish, which is achieved using a brush mop with the polishing machine, or small brush mop with the pendant motor. The remaining two will have a high, polished shine. Before these textures can be applied, the soldering and finishing must be completed.

MARKING AND PIERCING

STEP 1
Using a rule and dividers, mark nine equally spaced strips on the silver sheet. Each strip should be 3mm (⅛in) wide.

STEP 2
Cut the nine strips out of the sheet with the piercing saw, making the lines as straight as possible. File the edges until smooth. Then smooth all the pieces with emery paper.

STEP 3
Take two of the silver strips and texture them using the pin hammer and a flat plate. Hammer evenly and in the same direction on both pieces of silver so that they match.

MAKING AND FIXING JUMP RINGS

STEP 4
Use a narrow steel rod to make six jump rings, all the same size, for the tops of the silver strips. Hold the wire and rod in the vice and wrap the wire evenly round the rod until you have made enough rings. Cut the jump rings using the piercing saw. Using flat-nose pliers, bring the ends of the jump rings together.

STEP 5
To solder the jump rings onto the ends of the silver strips, cut several pallions of hard solder and brush flux all over the silver pieces. Melt a small piece of solder onto the end of a silver strip and then bring the jump ring to meet the silver strip. The solder will run and join the two. Repeat for each of the strips of silver.

TIP
The silver strips are larger than the small jump rings, so they will need more heat. Direct the flame towards the larger piece first until it reaches the correct temperature (pink, not red), then bring it toward the jump ring for the solder to join them together. Carefully hold the jump rings with heat-resistant tweezers.

STEP 6
Pickle and rinse all of the pieces. Rub the pieces that are not textured with dry emery paper to remove any fire stain. Emery the textured pieces on their reverse sides only, so as not to remove the texture. Make another, slightly larger jump ring for each strip using the end of a needlefile (if it is smooth enough) or another slightly larger steel rod. Using flat-nose pliers, thread these rings through the smaller rings and close the ends (right). Solder the joins with easy solder.

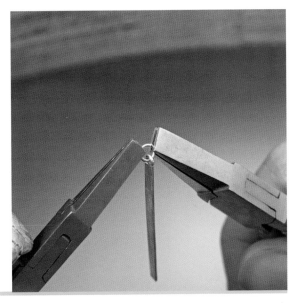

STEP 8
Make two large jump rings with the silver wire, about 1cm (⅜in) in diameter. Use the round-nose pliers or a steel rod of the appropriate width (depending on how large you want the jump ring to be) to do this. Thread the silver strips onto the larger jump rings. Join the ends of the jump rings with easy solder.

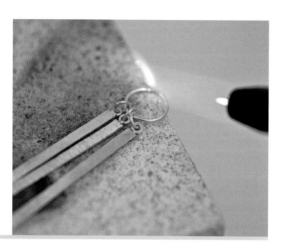

TIP
Keep the flame away from the silver strips and smaller jump rings by placing the piece to be soldered at the end of a soldering brick.

STEP 9
When the rings are attached, file away any excess solder. Polish the earrings with tripoli. Polish the textured strip and the plain, glossy strip with rouge. Holding the third strip away from the others, use the brush mop to give it a matt finish.

STEP 10
Make two earring wires with the 0.8mm (20-gauge) silver wire. Attach these to the finished earrings.

SEE ALSO
Piercing, page 30
Soldering, page 38
Finishing and polishing, page 42
Texturing, page 66
Making findings, page 86

TEXTURED BANGLE

A great piece for beginners, this project focuses on using bending, texturing and soldering techniques to make a simple bangle.

TOOLS AND MATERIALS

1mm (18-gauge) silver sheet: 22 x 1cm (8½ x ⅜in)

Wooden mallet

Piercing saw

Files

Soldering equipment

Emery papers

Ball pein hammer

Steel mandrel

Polishing equipment

TIP
Bend the silver into a slightly smaller ring than necessary, if possible. It will spring out a little, become a little bigger during the hammering process and so end up at the required size.

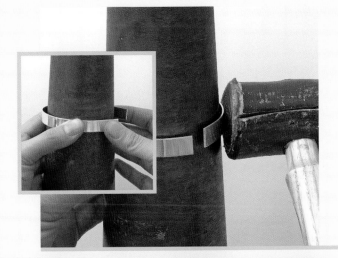

SHAPING THE BANGLE
STEP 1
Silver of this thickness is easy to bend without annealing. Bend the silver round the steel mandrel as far as possible using your fingers. A mallet may be useful to finish bending the ends completely round the mandrel.

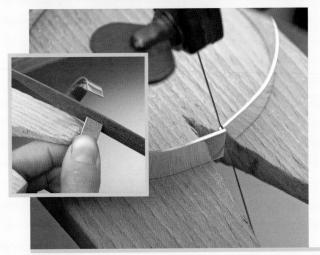

STEP 2
To fit the edges neatly together, cut them with a piercing saw to remove any uneven or overlapping silver. To do this, hold the bangle firmly on the peg and saw through both ends to ensure they fit together. If they do not meet perfectly, file the ends straight. The silver may still spring apart, so overlap the ends with your hands and then pull them back out again to meet.

STEP 3
Solder the ends of the bangle with hard solder. Place the solder on the inside of the bangle and draw it out with the heat from the flame, solder will always flow toward the heat. Pickle and rinse the bangle.

Place the solder on the inside of the bangle.

FILING AND TEXTURING

STEP 4 Remove any
excess solder from the bangle
at this stage. File it away with a
half-round file, using the flat side
on the outside of the bangle and
the rounded side of the file on the
inside of the bangle. Use emery
paper to smooth the filed area.

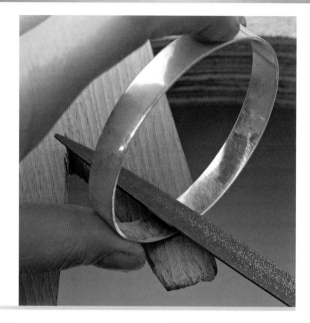

Hit the bangle straight
on when texturing.

STEP 5 Place the bangle
on the steel mandrel and use the
round end of the hammer to
create the texture. Take care to
hit flat against the bangle, not at
an angle, so as not to stretch it.
Make sure the texture is even all
round and that the bangle is
round in shape.

TIP

The ball pein hammer will give
a different texture from the
planishing hammer. Experiment
with a piece of brass first to be sure
of achieving the right texture.
The harder you hit, the more the
metal will spread, and this will
make the bangle larger in size.

STEP 6 Remove the
bangle from the steel mandrel
and file the inside, then rub with
emery paper. Polish to finish.

SEE ALSO
Filing, page 36
Soldering, page 38
Finishing and polishing, page 42
Texturing, page 66

DOMING

This is a terrific technique for creating three-dimensional shapes quickly and easily, and the resulting dome is a versatile shape. Joined in pairs they make a hollow bead. Domes can be used at the ends of a bangle, soldered onto a ring or in a wide variety of other jewellery.

MAKING DOMES

A doming block is used with doming punches of various sizes, domes can be soldered onto a piece singly, or joined to make a bead, or several domes can be combined in one design. Different coloured metals can be used for the dome and piece, for example when a dome is attached to a ring shank.

STARTING TO DOME

STEP 1 Start by choosing the dome size in the doming block and the punch to fit it, allowing space for the metal between the doming block and punch. Then score the size of the circle at the top edge of the doming block onto the metal. Pierce out the shape and anneal the metal. Place the metal disc onto the doming block. Make sure the metal is centred over the chosen dome hollow.

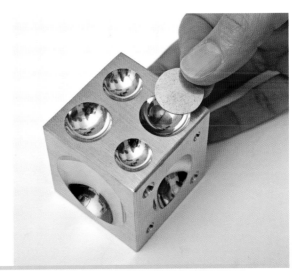

STEP 2 Hold the punch centred and vertical over the metal, and use a heavy hammer, for example the flat end of a ball pein hammer, to knock the punch into the metal. Move the metal round in the block, if necessary, and repeat the punching a few times to create a perfect dome.

Make sure the punch is centred on the metal.

MAKING A HIGHER DOME

Place the dome in the next smallest hollow in the doming block and repeat the hammering process. The sides of the dome will be higher and the dome smaller.

MAKING A HOLLOW BEAD

STEP 1 A hollow bead can be made by
punching two domes of the same size. File the edges of the domes until they are flat and fit together well.

STEP 2 Drill a hole in each dome before
soldering to prevent the air inside the bead from warming up. If the air becomes too hot, a perfect solder join will not be formed. Place the dome on a flat steel plate and tap a centre punch on the place you have marked for drilling a hole.

STEP 3 Move the dome to a wooden
block and drill a hole at the point marked by the punch. Punching the mark first provides some grip for the drill, and helps to prevent it from slipping as it begins to pierce the metal.

STEP 4 Place the domes on the soldering brick, brush well with flux, and place a few pieces of hard solder around the edge of one dome at regular intervals. Heat the dome until the solder has melted, but does not run too much.

Heat until you see the solder run.

STEP 5 Place the second dome on top of the first. Then heat gently until you can see the solder running around the join of the two domes.

STEP 6 Quench and pickle the bead, then rinse well to ensure that there is no pickle left inside it. File away any excess solder.

STEP 7
Emery and polish the bead. Here, a ring has been slipped through the drilled holes and then soldered to fix it securely.

PROFESSIONAL SAMPLE

This necklace uses different size domes as its main theme. Some of the domes have first been textured with a ball pein hammer.

SEE ALSO
Piercing, page 30
Drilling, page 34
Filing, page 36
Soldering, page 38
Finishing and polishing, page 42
Annealing, page 48

DOMED BRACELET

This stylish bracelet is constructed using a series of domed beads along with large jump rings. A toggle gives it an appropriate finishing touch because it is easily incorporated into the main design.

TOOLS AND MATERIALS

0.6mm (22-gauge)
silver sheet:
10 x 13.5cm (4 x 5½in)

0.8mm (20-gauge)
silver wire:
20cm (8in)

1mm (18-gauge)
silver wire:
30cm (12in)

1.2mm (16-gauge)
silver wire:
1cm (⅜in)

2mm (12-gauge)
silver wire:
3cm (1½in)

Soldering equipment

Dividers

Piercing saw

Files

Doming block and punches

Centre punch

Hammer or mallet

Drill

0.9mm (64-gauge) drill bit

Emery papers

Ring mandrel

Flat-nose and
round-nose pliers

Flat steel plate

Polishing equipment

STEP 1 Anneal the silver sheet, then pickle and rinse it. Open the dividers to 1cm (⅜in) and scribe six circles on the silver sheet, keeping them close together to avoid waste. Cut out the circles with the piercing saw and file their edges smooth.

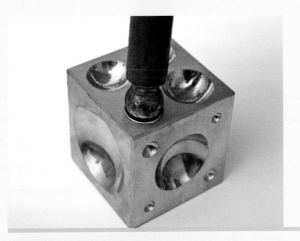

MAKING THE DOMES

STEP 2 Place a silver disk over the indent in the doming block that is slightly bigger than its circumference. Use the doming punch that fits the indent to hammer the disk into a dome, moving the punch all around the silver so that it forms an evenly shaped dome. Repeat with the remaining silver disks.

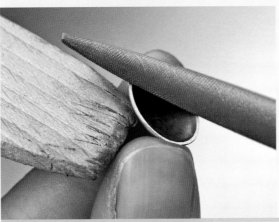

STEP 3 File the undersides of the domes until they are completely flat and take away any silver around the outside of the edge.

SOLDERING THE DOMES ONTO BASES

STEP 4 Soldering the domes onto bases will give them a more 'solid' appearance. It is easier to solder the domes on disks that are slightly larger than their diameter and cut off the excess afterward. Open the dividers about 1mm (¹⁄₁₆in) larger than for the first batch of circles and scribe circles on the silver sheet, allowing one for each dome. Pierce the disks out, but there is no need to file the edges.

STEP 5 When soldering hollow forms, the air inside expands with the heat, so it is necessary to drill holes first to allow the air to escape. In this design, the holes are used for the jump rings that join the links of the bracelet. Using a centre punch, mark two holes opposite each other on each flat silver disk, 2mm (1/16in) in from the edge. Then mark the domes in the same way, 2mm (1/16in) in from the edge. Drill all the holes with a 0.9mm (64-gauge) drill bit.

STEP 6 Prepare the domes and disks to be soldered by passing a gentle flame over them and brushing them with flux. Cut three small pieces of hard solder for each dome.

TIP
If there is a gap in the solder, it can be coaxed around using the heat of the torch, but do not overheat the piece.

STEP 7 Place a dome upside down on the soldering brick and place three pieces of solder evenly round the flat edge. Heat until the solder has just melted. Turn the dome over and place it centrally on a disk. Heat all the metal evenly until you can see the solder running all the way round.

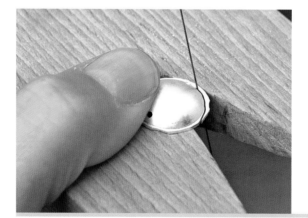

STEP 8 Solder the remaining domes to disks, then pickle and rinse them very well. When they are dry, pierce the excess silver from round the edge of the dome. Then file the edge and rub it with emery paper.

MAKING LARGE JUMP RINGS

STEP 9 Secure the ring mandrel in the vice. Bend the 18-gauge (1mm) wire round the top of the mandrel by hand until the wire overlaps. Remove the wire from the mandrel and cut the ring off with the piercing saw.

Repeat to make six rings. Bring the ends of each ring together using flat-nose pliers and solder them with hard solder. Pickle and rinse. File away any lumps of solder.

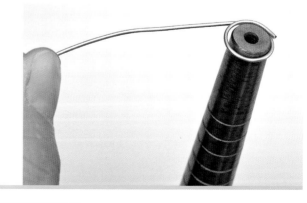

STEP 10 Place a ring on a flat steel plate. Tap gently with the flat end of a hammer to flatten the ring. Repeat with the remaining rings. Rub the rings with emery paper.

SEE ALSO
Piercing, page 30
Drilling, page 34
Filing, page 36
Soldering, page 38
Finishing and polishing, page 42
Doming, page 75
Making findings, page 86

STEP 11 Use 12-gauge (2mm) wire to make the toggle clasp. Cut 1.5cm (¾in) and 5mm (¼in) lengths. File the ends flat and solder the pieces together in a T-shape using hard solder. Use round-nose pliers to make a small jump ring. Solder the ring on the small end of the toggle. File and emery all over.

STEP 12 Make twelve jump rings using 20-gauge (0.8mm) wire, about 5mm (¼in) in diameter. Cut the rings apart and place them in the vent holes in the domes. Link the domes using the large rings. Be sure to have a large ring at one end and the toggle at the other end. Close the ends of the rings and solder each one with easy solder. Pickle, rinse and dry the bracelet, then polish it with tripoli and rouge.

RIVETING

Riveting is a versatile technique that is both practical for joining metal and useful as a decorative effect. It is a great way to join metal without soldering, adding movement by using one rivet or colour when selecting a different metal for the rivets. It adds another dimension to a piece of work. Of course, it can also be used to join different materials, such as metal and wood, plastic or paper.

CREATIVE RIVETING

To make the rivet part of the design that will stand out and be noticed, use a different metal, such as copper wire when joining silver. It is not necessary to have to rivet flush against the piece – it can be raised slightly, by not tapping it down so far, and rounded off with a file.

Metal tubing can be used to make rivets. Select tubing the same size as the hole, but instead of tapping it down with a pin hammer, use a pointed punch inside the tube to spread it out round the hole, and then tap it down. To make a piece of jewellery with a rivet at each corner, first drill a hole or holes for the rivets. Then use wire that is the same diameter as the holes, not too small as it will not hold tightly enough.

PREPARING THE RIVETS

STEP 1 For riveting, use wire the same size as the hole you are going to drill, here, 1.5mm (14-gauge) wire is used. It is easier to spread one end of the wire before putting it through the hole, so place it vertically in a vice, using protectors to prevent the teeth of the vice from damaging the wire. Have a generous amount, round 3–4mm (⅛in) of the wire above the top of the vice.

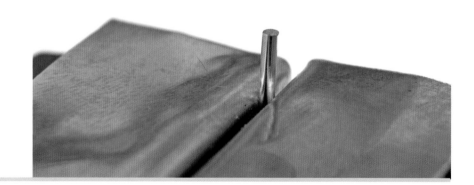

STEP 2 Using the flat end of a pin hammer, tap the top end of the wire until it is spread enough not to fall through the hole.

JOINING WITH RIVETS

STEP 1 Tape the pieces to be joined together with masking tape, so that they do not move as you work. Push the wire through the holes of the pieces to be joined together. With the spread end of the wire underneath, place the piece on a flat steel plate or anvil so that the wire will not fall out. Use a pair of end cutters to snip the wire, leaving about 2–3mm (⅛in) above the hole.

STEP 2 File the end of the wire so it is flat.

STEP 3 Spread the end of the wire with the pin hammer to create a rivet that holds the pieces together.

STEP 4 If there is any excess metal wire protruding, file it away and the rivet will hardly be noticed. Alternatively, the rivet can be left slightly protruding on the surface as a feature.

SEE ALSO
Drilling, page 34
Forging, page 58

RIVETED CUFFLINKS

Riveting can be used to join metal and other materials without soldering. For these cufflinks, the technique is used to join silver elements with silver rivets, focusing on the rivets as part of the design.

TOOLS AND MATERIALS

0.6mm (22-gauge) silver sheet: 3cm (1¼in) square

0.8mm (20-gauge) silver wire: 5cm (2in)

Steel rule

Scribe

Piercing saw

Drill

1mm (61-gauge) drill bit

Files

Flat steel plate

Pin hammer

Soldering equipment

Dividers

Silver cufflink fittings

Polishing equipment

Centre punch

SEE ALSO

Piercing, page 30
Drilling, page 34
Filing, page 36
Soldering, page 38
Finishing and polishing, page 42
Texturing, page 66
Riveting, page 82

STEP 1
Mark the sheet into quarters with a steel rule and scribe. Cut in half using the piercing saw. Then cut one half into two and set these small squares aside. Leave the other half intact as it is easier to drill out the centres when there is more metal to hold.

STEP 2
Using the dividers, scribe circles in the two joined squares, leaving an edge of at least 3mm (⅛in) round the circles at the narrowest points. Drill small holes in two places near the inside of the circles and pierce the circles out. Pierce on the inside of the scribed lines to ensure the circles do not get too big.

STEP 3
Cut the silver sheet in half to make two squares with circle cut-outs. File the edges of all four squares with a flat file until smooth. File the inner edges of the circles with a half-round file.

TEXTURING THE SQUARES
STEP 4
Place one of the solid squares on the flat plate. Using the pointed end of the pin hammer, hammer the silver all over in the same direction to create a distinct and even texture. Repeat with the other square.

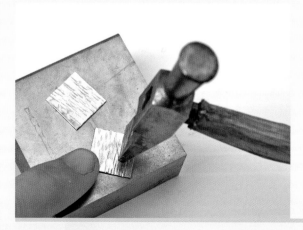

SOLDERING

STEP 5
Solder the cufflink fittings onto the untextured sides of the solid squares using hard solder, having first fluxed both surfaces well. Hold the cufflink fitting with heat-resistant tweezers, grasping the arm of the fitting, not the hollow bar, which would collapse with the heat. Melt a piece of solder on the end of the cufflink fitting.

STEP 6
Gently heat the silver square and hold the cufflink fitting in place until the solder runs. Repeat with the other square and fitting. Pickle, rinse and dry the pieces, then rub the underside of each piece with emery paper. Take care to avoid damaging the hollow bar. Polish all the silver pieces while they are separate.

DRILLING AND RIVETING

STEP 7
Place the squares with circles cut out on top of the textured squares and hold them together firmly with masking tape. Use a pencil to mark a point 2mm (1/16in) in from each corner for drilling rivet holes. Use a centre punch to make a permanent mark and then drill each hole carefully using a 1mm (61-gauge) drill bit.

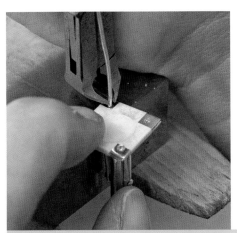

STEP 8
Rivet the cufflinks together. Make sure the top of each rivet is the same size and cut all the rivets to the same length, 2mm (1/16in), before hammering. When the rivets have been hammered flat, file them smooth on each side.

POLISHING

STEP 9
Polish again with rouge to finish the cufflinks. Wash the cufflinks well with detergent and a soft toothbrush to remove the rouge from inside the fittings.

MAKING FINDINGS

Findings is the jewellery term for clasps, hooks, jump rings, cufflink fittings and so on, that can be bought ready-made. Some items, such as cufflink fittings with springs inside them, are very difficult and time-consuming to make, but there are others that can be made easily. If bought items cannot be made to your specification, 'fittings' for them are made by hand.

VERSATILE JUMP RINGS

One of the most useful, frequently used fittings is the jump ring, which can be made from any thickness of wire and any size ring. To make several jump rings the same size, all you need is some wire, a rod the same diameter as the required jump rings, a vice and a saw. The smooth end of a needlefile is a useful size, or you can use nails, or find other suitable rods. They must be smooth.

Once a jump ring is soldered, it is easy to change its shape, for example into an oval. Simply place both ends of a pair of round-nose pliers inside the soldered jump ring and gently open the pliers. The jump ring will become oval. Jump rings can be flattened with a hammer on a flat steel plate.

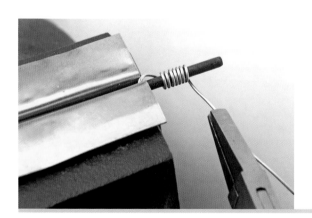

MAKING JUMP RINGS

STEP 1 Place the rod and the wire in the vice so they are held tightly together. Hold the wire, using pliers if the wire is thick, and wind it round the rod, pulling tightly so that the wire looks like a spring round the rod. When you have made enough rings, cut the wire with end cutters, and take the rod and wire out of the vice.

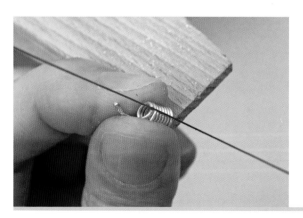

STEP 2 To cut the jump rings from the coil, hold it firmly against the pin. Using a piercing saw, cut them away starting at the top or bottom, whichever feels more comfortable. To saw a few jump rings off at once, pierce the coil in a straight line. The rings will collect at the bottom of the saw frame, or fall off into the bench skin.

STEP 3
To put the ends of a jump ring together ready for soldering, hold each end in a pair of flat-nose pliers and bring them together until they meet.

EARRING POSTS

Earring posts are also easy to make with wire. The most common thickness of ear wire is 0.8mm (20-gauge). To make an earring post for an ear stud, cut the required length, usually about 1cm (½in) and file each end flat.

The groove often found on earring posts to hold the scroll (the butterfly that holds the earring on your ear) in place is made using a square needlefile. Rest the post on the pin and hold the file at a right angle, about three-fourths of the way up. Turn the post as you file the groove to make sure it is even all round.

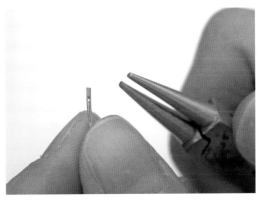

Instead of filing grooves into a earring post, squeeze it with round-nose pliers.

EARRING WIRES

Earring wires are more difficult to make than jump rings. It can take some practice with pliers to bend wire to be able to make two earring hooks the same. Use the same thickness wire as the posts. Cut about 8cm (3½in) wire, or longer if you prefer longer hooks, and file the ends flat and smooth.

MAKING EARRING WIRES

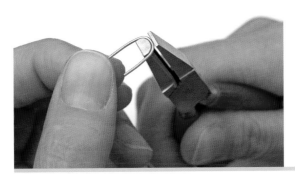

STEP 1
Hold a pair of half-round pliers about halfway along the wire and bend the wire, with the rounded end of the pliers on the inside of the bend.

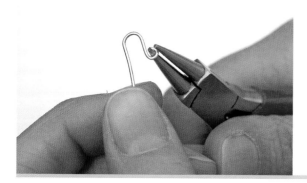

STEP 2
Using a pair of round-nose pliers, hold the wire at one end, and bend it into a small ring.

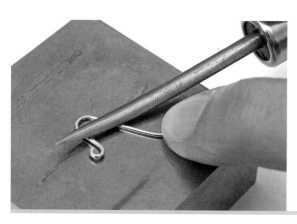

STEP 3
Use half-round pliers to bend the other end of the wire out at a slight curve.

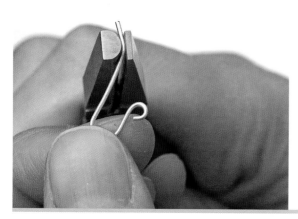

STEP 4
Harden the earring hook with a burnisher on a flat steel plate or hammer it very gently with the flat end of a pin hammer.

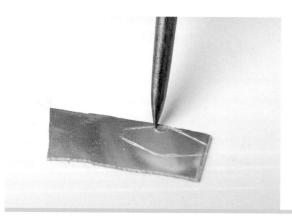

MAKING A BALE
STEP 1
To make a bale for the top of a pendant, use a silver sheet, about 3mm (8-gauge) thick. Draw the shape of the bale on a piece of paper, and then draw it as it would be opened up. Transfer this drawing to the metal sheet.

STEP 2
Cut out the shape with a piercing saw and file the edges.

SEE ALSO
Piercing, page 30
Soldering, page 38
Using wire, page 50
Bending, page 64

STEP 3
Using half-round pliers, bend the metal until the thinner ends meet.

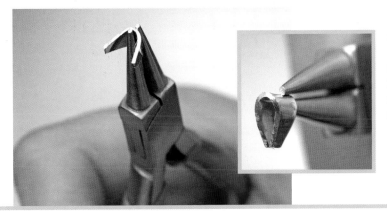

STEP 4
Solder the ends of the bale: it is then ready to solder onto the piece.

PROFESSIONAL SAMPLES
Below are some examples of findings in use on finished pieces: bales soldered to pendants (bottom, left); earring posts soldered to earrings (top, left); jump rings soldered to earrings (centre); and ear wires attached directly to earrings (right).

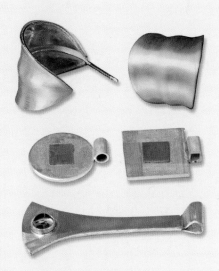

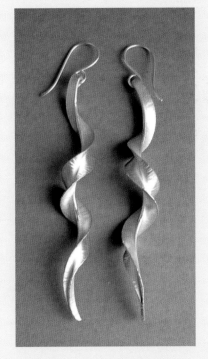

RUB-OVER SETTING

There are many types of setting for holding stones in place in jewellery, this one is commonly used for cabochon stones, which are smooth, with a flat bottom and rounded top. Every stone is individual in width and depth, and each setting is made for a particular stone. The setting can be soldered onto any piece, such as a ring, pendant, brooch or cufflink.

SETTINGS AND STONES

A rub-over setting is so named because the fine wire to make the setting is literally 'rubbed over' the stone with a pusher, a tool designed for this purpose. Making settings, and setting stones, can be difficult, so it is a good idea to make your first setting for a large, oval or round stone, and progress to smaller settings as you gradually master the technique and feel confident.

SELECTING SEMIPRECIOUS STONES
Choosing stones for your jewellery is fun. There are so many colours and shapes of stones that are readily available and relatively inexpensive. When you are just beginning to make jewellery with set stones, think about the size and shape before you design. A large oval or round stone (cabochon) is the easiest shape. Once you are confident about making settings, you can be more adventurous with sizes and shapes. Try to choose stones that have a flat bottom and are quite even in shape, with shoulders that are not too high or low. An uneven bottom will not sit flat in the setting.

BEZEL WIRE

Jewellers use fine silver or gold wire, known as bezel wire, to make the top part of the casing for a stone. This wire is very thin, and therefore malleable; it can be shaped with the fingers alone, although pliers do give a more even result. However, due to its thinness, it can also be dented easily with the pliers, and melted easily while soldering, so great care is necessary.

MEASURING MATERIALS

The size of stone determines the length of wire and dimensions of the silver sheet required. The bezel wire should be long enough to fit round the stone, with a little excess. The sheet of silver should be 2–3mm ($\frac{1}{16}$–$\frac{1}{8}$in) larger than the stone. For example, the stone used in this example is 7 x 4mm ($\frac{1}{4}$ x $\frac{3}{16}$in) and the silver sheet is 10 x 6mm ($\frac{3}{8}$ x $\frac{1}{4}$in).

MAKING A RUB-OVER SETTING

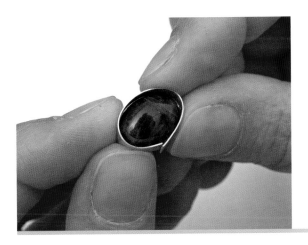

STEP 1 Select the stone for the piece, then bend the bezel wire round the stone with your fingers until it overlaps. On an oval stone ensure the join is on the longer side of the stone. The setting size is important: the stone should drop into the setting from above without having to be pushed, but it must not rattle loosely when in place.

STEP 2 When the size is right, cut the wire, and solder the join together with hard solder. Be sure to place the solder on the outside of the join as any solder remaining on the inside will reduce the size of the setting.

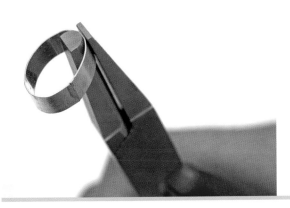

STEP 3 After soldering, quench and pickle the wire and rinse it. Then use half-round pliers to shape the wire perfectly to the stone.

TIP

For precious stones it is worth using a setter, someone who specialises in setting stones. Different stones have different qualities, some are harder, others softer, and they react differently to polish or the ultrasonic machine. Ask the supplier for information on the stone's properties.

STEP 4 File the bottom of the bezel wire to ensure it will sit flat on the base. Then solder the bezel onto the base, placing several pieces of hard solder round the edge.

TIP
As the bezel wire is usually thinner than the base, it is a good idea to pick up the work with heat-resistant tweezers, and heat it from underneath. Watch the solder run all the way round the setting.

STEP 5 Pickle and rinse the setting after soldering. Then cut away the excess silver with a piercing saw and file the edge until smooth. Take care not to pierce or file into the fine bezel wire. Flux both the setting and the piece it is to be attached to and solder the setting onto the piece.

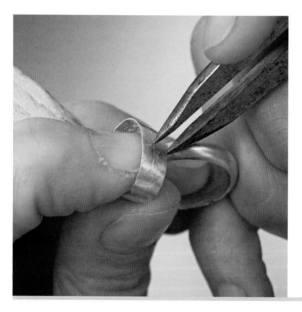

STEP 6 Trim the bezel wire until just enough metal covers the stone to hold it in place. The metal needs to extend just over the first section of the slope. As each stone varies, this trimming process is completely individual; at a guess, two-thirds of the height usually remains. Mark the height for trimming and use dividers to scribe a line round the setting. Then cut off the excess with a piercing saw and file the cut edge flat. Clean and polish the setting.

SEE ALSO
Piercing, page 30
Filing, page 36
Soldering, page 38
Finishing and polishing, page 42
Directory of gems, page 116

STEP 7

Place the stone into the setting and hold the piece very tightly using a ring clamp. Use a pusher to push the metal gently over the stone, starting at one side, then work on the opposite side. Then work in between the first two places, and finally work all round the stone. Press a little more firmly and go round again. Keep working until the metal is evenly over the stone and holding it firmly in place. If necessary, take away any small bumps with fine emery paper.

STEP 8

Use a burnisher to smooth the metal and polish the setting with rouge if necessary.

PROFESSIONAL SAMPLES

These bezel-set rings show something of the range of colours, sizes and shapes of cabochons that are available. Making use of this broad range of stones can make a selection of rings with very simple and similar shanks look very different to each other.

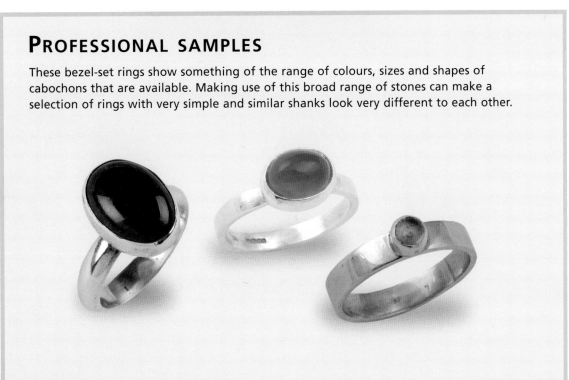

PENDANT WITH RUB-OVER SETTING

Rub-over settings can be used to decorate many items, in this case a simply-shaped pendant. Keep it simple by using a round or oval semiprecious stone.

TOOLS AND MATERIALS

1mm (18-gauge) silver sheet: 4 x 2cm (1½ x ¾in)

0.6mm (22-gauge) silver sheet: 2cm (¾in) square

Piercing saw

Files

Bezel wire

Stone

Soldering equipment

Emery papers

Bale (see page 88)

Polishing equipment

Dividers

PIERCING THE PENDANT

STEP 1 Draw the design on a piece of tracing paper with a pen. Adhere the paper firmly onto the 1mm (18-gauge) silver sheet with double-sided tape. Cut round the shape with the piercing saw. File the edge until smooth.

MAKING THE SETTING

STEP 2 Make the setting for the stone with bezel wire and 0.6mm (22-gauge) silver sheet.

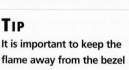

STEP 3 Use hard solder to solder the bezel wire to the base of the setting. Smooth the base of the setting with a flat file ready for soldering onto the pendant. Solder the setting on the silver pendant, using easy solder to avoid melting the solder in the setting. Melt a small piece of easy solder onto the bottom of the setting. Put the setting in place on the pendant. Hold the silver with heat-resistant tweezers and apply the flame underneath the pendant. Pickle and rinse.

TIP

It is important to keep the flame away from the bezel wire, which is so thin that it can melt easily. Using the flame of the torch underneath the piece when soldering an item of this type ensures the bezel wire gets as little heat as possible.

FIXING THE BALE

STEP 4 Make the bale
for the pendant. When the
ends of the bale have been
soldered together, use the
rounded side of a half-round
file to shape the sides of the
bale to fit the pendant. Solder
the bale onto the pendant
with easy solder.

Pickle and rinse. File all the
edges of the pendant smooth.
Rub the pendant with emery
papers and polish with tripoli.

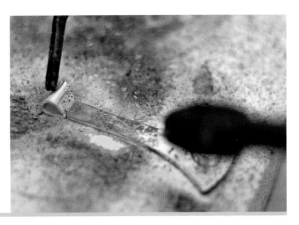

CUTTING DOWN THE BEZEL WIRE

STEP 5 The height of
the setting needs to be reduced.
Hold the stone to the side of the
setting to judge where to cut, and
mark all round the setting with
dividers. Pierce carefully with the
saw and file flat.

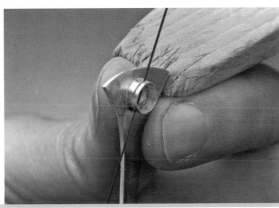

STEP 6 Gently file an
angle round the setting and place
the stone in the setting.
Set the stone with the pusher.

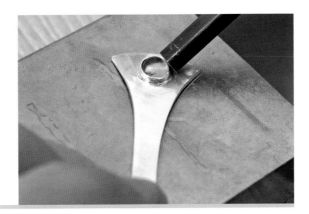

STEP 7 Smooth the rub-
over setting with the burnisher.
Polish with rouge and rinse well.

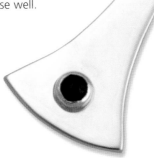

SEE ALSO
Piercing, page 30
Soldering, page 38
Finishing and polishing, page 42
Making findings, page 86
Rub-over setting, page 90
Directory of gems, page 116

LINK BRACELET

For this piece, a bracelet, you will use several of the techniques covered in the book: piercing, texturing, drilling, reticulation, filing and polishing. You can add more links to make a necklace instead. Each link is the same shape and size, but each one has a different design or finish.

TOOLS AND MATERIALS

1.2mm (16-gauge) silver sheet: 1.5 x 10.5cm (⅝ x 4in)

0.8mm (20-gauge) silver round wire: 20cm (8in)

1mm (18-gauge) silver round wire: 20cm (8in)

Steel rule

Scribe

Dividers

Piercing saw

Files

Drill and drill bits

Soldering equipment

Centre punch

Rolling mill

Vice and rods

Flat-nose pliers

Emery papers

Catches or bolt rings

Polishing equipment

CUTTING AND FILING

STEP 1 Start by measuring 1.5cm (⅝in) squares along the silver sheet, using the dividers, or scribe and rule. You can use a steel square to be sure of the 90 degree angles. Cut out the squares with the piercing saw.

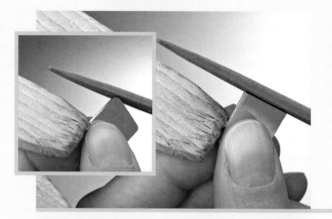

STEP 2 File each square carefully so as not to lose the shape. Gently file curves into each corner to soften the squares. Put aside two squares: later, one square will be polished to a high shine and another will have a matt finish created by a satin mop.

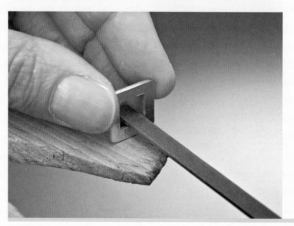

DRILLING AND PIERCING

STEP 3 Using the steel rule and scribe, measure a smaller square inside one of the larger ones. Mark and punch where to drill, then drill a small hole on the inside of the smaller square and pierce the shape out. File the inside so it looks perfectly square. Try to keep the corners straight; use a square needlefile if necessary.

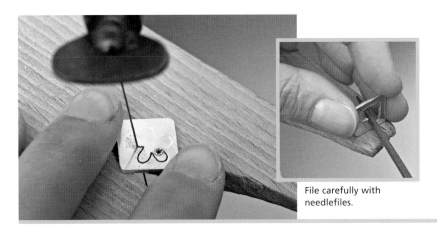

SOLDERING

STEP 4
Draw a flower or starfish design on a piece of tracing paper. Stick this to another of the silver squares with double-sided tape. Drill a small hole on the inside of the flower, and, as in Step 3, pierce out the flower and file carefully with needlefiles.

File carefully with needlefiles.

STEP 5
One square has several drilled holes of various sizes. Mark carefully where they will be and punch an indent. Use a 0.9mm (64-gauge) bit to drill all the holes. Change to a 1mm (61-gauge) bit and drill again, leaving a couple of holes at the smaller size. Change to a 1.2mm (56-gauge) bit and drill a few larger holes. The holes should get larger in the row or circle within the square.

You could use anything you like to texture one of the silver squares, here sequin waste has been used.

TEXTURING

STEP 6
Use the rolling mill (see page 68) and a textured item to create texture in the next silver square. This square will probably need to be flattened between two flat steel plates, or with a mallet, and refiled round the edges to make it perfectly square again.

STEP 7 The final square will be textured by reticulation (see page 67). Place it on the soldering brick and flux well. Pass the soldering torch over it until the surface begins to melt to create the texture desired. This square may also need to be flattened and refiled round the edges.

Use reticulation to texture one of the squares.

A reticulated square.

STEP 8 Using the 0.8mm (20-gauge) wire, make enough small jump rings to be able to solder four onto each square. Cut them and bring the ends together neatly. Make more jump rings with the 1mm (18-gauge) wire, but leave them open for now.

STEP 9 Solder the small jump rings onto the squares, making sure the joins of the jump rings are on the soldered side. Use hard solder. Try to solder them as evenly as possible.

Position the jump rings as evenly as possible.

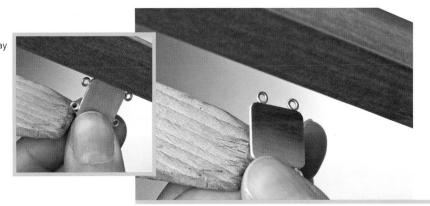

File away any excess solder.

STEP 10 When all the squares have been pickled, rinsed and dried, file away any excess solder and emery each square all over with both grades of paper.

STEP 11 Join the squares with the larger jump rings. Solder them with easy solder, holding each ring up away from the bracelet with the heat-resistant tweezers. This may be tricky, but try to keep the heat away from the square links and small jump rings. Finish one end with two large jump rings and the other with two S-hooks or bolt rings.

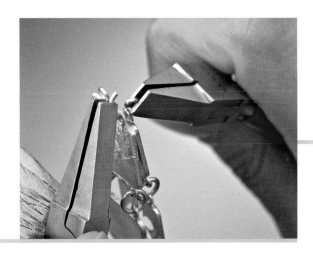

Hold the jump rings away from the bracelet as you solder.

STEP 12 Finally, polish the whole bracelet with tripoli. Carefully use the satin mop on the one link that will have the matt finish. Then use rouge on the rest of the bracelet, keeping the one matt square link away from the mop.

SEE ALSO
Piercing, page 30
Drilling, page 34
Filing, page 36
Soldering, page 38
Finishing and polishing, page 42
Texturing, page 66
Making findings, page 86

Using beads

Techniques used for making beaded jewellery can be adapted to a number of styles. Some semiprecious beads are threaded with knots separating each bead. This stops the beads from rubbing against each other, and also prevents you from losing all the beads if the thread breaks. Other useful methods are crimping, for securing the end of a necklace, using calottes to cover unsightly knots or crimps and making secure wire loops for earrings or multistrand necklaces.

Knotting using two strands

Using the two threads together, attach a calotte (see page 102) to the end of the thread. Thread both needles through a bead and push the bead up to the calotte. Take one thread in each hand and form an overhand knot up against the bead, repeat to the desired length, and then thread on a calotte and knot the threads right up against the calotte, using a double knot. Put on a dot of glue and close the calotte. To complete the necklace, close the loop on the calotte round the hole in the clasp.

Knotting using a single strand

Step 1
Attach a needle to a length of beading silk. Attach a knot cover to the end of the silk. Thread on a bead. Form an overhand knot, keeping the knot loose.

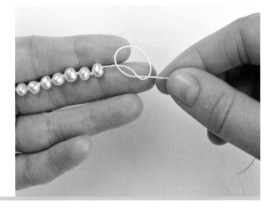

Step 2
Insert a darning needle or awl into the knot and slide the knot towards the bead. Only remove the needle when the knot is snug against the bead. Take care when tightening the knot. Repeat for the length of the necklace. This method needs practice in order to produce knots that are snug against the beads.

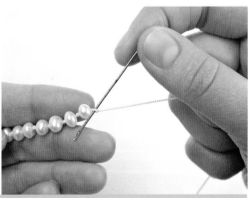

CRIMPING

STEP 1 Crimps are useful for securing the ends of necklaces. The easiest crimps to use are 2mm (¹⁄₁₆in) tubes. Cut a length of beading wire that is 10cm (4in) longer than the length of the necklace. Thread one end through the crimp, then through the hole in the clasp, and back through the crimp. Position the crimp so that you have 5cm (2in) of spare wire left as a tail. Move the crimp up towards the clasp, but leave enough space for the clasp to move freely.

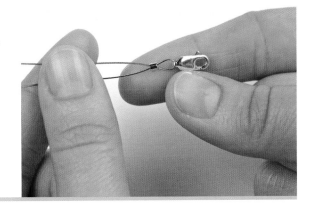

STEP 2 Place the threaded crimp bead into the groove in the crimping pliers that is nearest to the handle and squeeze gently. You will see that the crimp is now U-shaped, with a little channel running along its length.

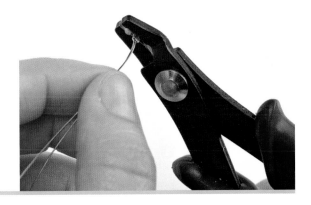

STEP 3 Give the crimp bead a quarter turn so that the channel is on the side, and insert it into the front groove of the pliers. Gently squeeze the pliers so that the crimp forms a rounded tube shape.

The crimp will form a rounded tube shape.

A crimp securing the end of a necklace.

STEP 4 String the beads onto the long length of wire. String the 5cm (2in) tail through the first few beads for security and then cut the tail close to the bead. Repeat at the other end of the necklace. Alternatively, crimps can be flattened with flat-nose pliers, but this gives a less polished look.

CRIMP COVERS

STEP 1 Crimp covers give
a stylish finish to jewellery. Slide the
crimp cover over the crimp. Hold it
in the front section of the crimping
pliers so that the gap in the cover
faces forwards.

Squeeze the crimp cover
closed over the crimp.

STEP 2 Gently squeeze the
cover with the pliers until it forms a
round bead. Do not squeeze too hard
or the cover will buckle and collapse.

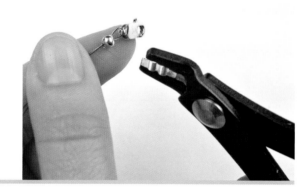

USING CALOTTES

STEP 1 Some calottes have a hole
between the two cups, while others just clamp
round the knot. String the beads onto beading
wire. Thread on the calotte so that the cup faces
the end of the necklace.

STEP 2 Make a large knot in the end of
the wire by winding it round your finger and
passing the end through twice. Insert a needle
into the knot before it is pulled tight and slide
the knot up against the calotte.

STEP 3
Put a little glue or nail polish on the knot to prevent it from opening. Squeeze the two cup-shaped halves of the calotte together with pliers.

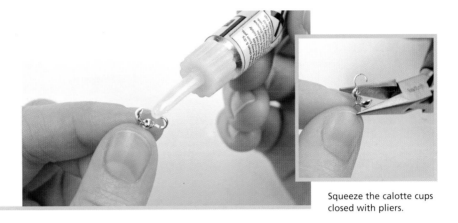

Squeeze the calotte cups closed with pliers.

STEP 4
Insert the loop of the calotte into the clasp and close the loop. Repeat at the other end of the necklace.

A calotte gives a neat finish to a necklace.

SIMPLE WIRE LOOP

STEP 1
Simple loops are a good choice for beginners and are ideal for securing a few beads on an earring. Position a pair of flat-nose pliers about 8mm (⁵⁄₁₆in) from the end of the wire and bend the wire away from you at a right angle.

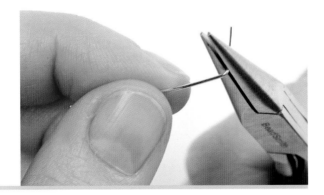

SEE ALSO
Using wire, page 50
Making findings, page 86

STEP 2 Grasp the wire a few millimetres from the bend with the round-nose pliers. Turn the pliers anticlockwise until about half of the loop is formed (a turn of about 90 degrees).

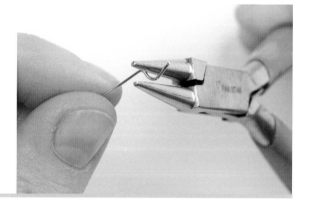

A finished simple loop.

STEP 3 Now grasp the end of the wire with the pliers and pull it round to finish the loop. Try to keep the loop as round as possible. Trim off any excess wire. This loop is fine for earrings with a few beads, but for a more secure loop, or for heavier beads, use a wrapped loop.

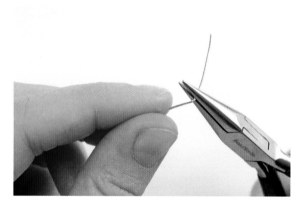

WRAPPED LOOP

STEP 1 A wrapped loop gives a more secure and professional finish than a simple loop. Position a pair of flat-nose pliers about 2–3mm (¹⁄₁₆–¹⁄₈in) from the end of the wire and bend the wire away from you at a right angle. Change to a pair of round-nose pliers and grasp the wire on the short end next to the bend. Bend the short end round the pliers with your fingers to form a loop.

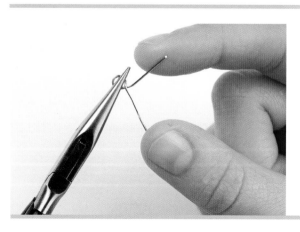

STEP 2 Change the pliers to your other hand and hold the loop. Using your fingers or the half-round pliers, begin wrapping the short wire round the long wire for three or more turns.

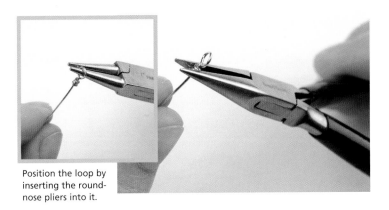

Position the loop by inserting the round-nose pliers into it.

STEP 3 Cut the wire and press down the sharp end. If necessary insert the round-nose pliers into the loop to position it correctly (shown left).

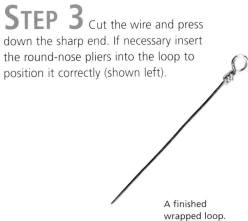

A finished wrapped loop.

PROFESSIONAL SAMPLES

Many types of semiprecious stones are supplied with drill holes, and in many different shapes, so it is possible to make simple yet visually exciting pieces with beads. Below, many different types of stone have been used in one necklace. Right, petal-shaped beads have been used in conjunction with delicate metallic leaf shapes.

STRUNG NECKLACE

This necklace is made with a strand of faceted amethyst beads, but you can use any drilled bead or pearl.

The technique of knotting between each bead is most often used where the value of the beads is high.

It also makes the necklace more flexible and looks attractive, especially when a contrasting colour thread is used.

TOOLS AND MATERIALS

1 string of drilled stones

Pearl silk or nylon thread four times the length you want the necklace to be

Fine threading or beading needle

2cm (¾in) of gimp (metal tubing made from very thin coiled wire and bought ready-made) in a colour that matches the clasp and catch

A clasp with jump rings

Clear nail polish

End cutters

STEP 1
However long you want your necklace to be, use four times that length of threading silk or nylon. This will allow you to knot between each bead for extra security should the necklace break. Thread the silk or nylon onto the needle, and take the needle to the middle of the thread so you have a double strand.

STEP 2
Gimp will strengthen thread where it passes through the clasp. Cut the length of gimp in half. String three beads and then a piece of gimp onto the thread, followed by one of the rings on the clasp. Pull these down to about 10cm (4in) from one end of the thread.

SEE ALSO
Using beads, page 100
Multistrand necklace, page 108

STEP 3
Holding the short end of the thread taut, pass the needle back through the first bead, as shown. Pull the thread tight so the gimp forms a loop round the ring of the clasp.

STEP 4
Use the long end of the thread to tie a knot round the shorter end. Pull it tight against the first bead.

STEP 5
Pass a needle through the next bead and tie another knot. Do the same with the third bead.

STEP 6
Next, string another bead onto the long end of the thread and tie a loose knot in it (the short end of the thread will be trimmed later). Work the knot along with your finger or a needle until it is close to the bead, then open out the two threads to tighten the knot snugly against the last bead. Repeat the knotting process to add more beads until only three beads remain.

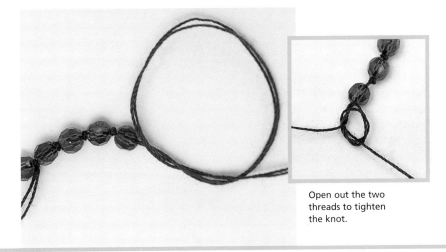

Open out the two threads to tighten the knot.

STEP 7
String on the last three beads without knotting them, then a piece of gimp, and finally the ring at the other end of the clasp. Pass the needle back through the last bead and pull tight. This should tighten up the whole necklace and close the gimp round the ring of the clasp. Tie a knot between the last two beads with the loose piece of thread. Repeat this process between the next two pairs of beads.

STEP 8
If you have used silk thread, finish the necklace by putting a tiny dot of clear nail polish onto the three knots at each end of the necklace and trimming off the excess thread with a pair of end cutters when the polish is dry.

MULTISTRAND NECKLACE

This project specifies three 40cm (15¾in) strands of amethysts and silver beads, but you can substitute different semiprecious beads. You can also alter the length of the necklace and the size of the beads to suit your own taste.

TOOLS AND MATERIALS

Flexible beading wire

1 string 5mm drilled amethyst rounds

2 strings 5–7mm amethyst ovals

10 x 10mm amethyst disks

40 x 2mm silver beads

25 x 3mm silver beads

0.8mm (20-gauge) silver wire: 20cm (8in)

Flat-nose and round-nose pliers

2 silver cones

1 S-shaped silver clasp

STRINGING THE BEADS

STEP 1
Cut three strands of flexible beading wire the length of your finished necklace plus 12cm (4¾in). Arrange the beads on a bead board and string the three strands. Reserve two 3mm silver beads to cover the end of the cone. Tape the ends of the beading wire with masking tape so that you don't lose your beads.

STEP 2
Cut two lengths of silver wire about 10cm (4in) long and make a wrapped loop at one end of each wire (see page 104).

JOINING THE STRANDS

STEP 3
Take the first strand of beads and attach to a wrapped loop with crimps (see page 101). Thread the short end of the beading wire back through several beads, and cut the wire close to the bead. Repeat for the other two strands of beads.

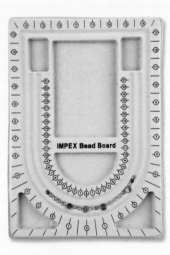

BEAD BOARD
A beading design board can be used to set out your beads before you string them; that way if a design isn't working you can start again without taking the necklace apart.

Attach all strands of the necklace to the wrapped loop using crimps.

STEP 4
Thread the silver wire through the cone so that the cone covers the crimps and wrapped loop. Thread on a silver bead and make a wrapped loop at the other end, large enough for the S-shaped clasp to go through.

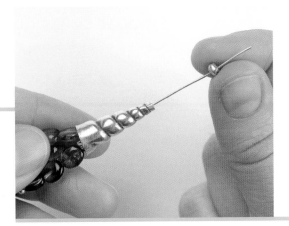

STEP 5
Repeat Step 4 at the other end of the necklace.

STEP 6
Thread the S-shaped clasp through each loop to fasten the necklace.

SEE ALSO
Making findings, page 86
Using beads, page 100

CHAPTER 3
RESOURCES

The resources chapter contains a wealth of useful information, from ideas on shapes for all kinds of jewellery to handy information on gemstones and their qualities. There is also a guide to metals and melting points, conversion charts, a glossary of terms and a list of useful sources of information such as websites, books and magazines.

IDEA FILE: SHAPES

The range of shapes and forms in which a piece of jewellery can be made is virtually infinite. The following pages are illustrated with a variety of designs to represent a basic spectrum of shapes for the beginner.

RINGS

PARALLEL BANDS

It is easier to pass a narrow parallel band over a knuckle than a wide one. Indeed, a wide band may need to be made at least a size larger than a narrow one to fit over the same finger. Remember that temperature affects finger size.

TAPERED BANDS

Tapering can be used to draw attention to a focal point, and to reduce both visual and material weight. Tapering a wide ring to a narrow base can also be a method of reducing potential discomfort to the wearer.

STONE SET

Stones set in rings can be subject to a great deal of wear, and can be vulnerable to damage; the choice of stone and setting should thus be carefully considered. The depth of the stone may dictate the thickness of the band.

EARRINGS

STUDS

The position of the post must be carefully considered, so that the stud does not tilt away from the ear due to an imbalance of weight. If the earring's form is too deep, this may also cause tilting.

EAR WIRES

Consider the length of the ear wires. If they are too short, the earrings can be accidentally pushed out of the lobe. Solid ear wires on drop earrings can be vulnerable in that the ear wire is more likely to break off.

Necklaces

Simple

Simple need not mean dull so long as sufficient attention is paid to detail. Subtle details such as relief can add to the three-dimensional quality of a form without appearing overstated. The finish of a piece can also draw attention to the detail.

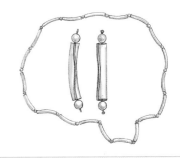

Long

Long necklaces can easily be passed over the head, so they generally do not need to have a clasp. Length can also create versatility; doubling-up a piece will create a different look and effect than when it is worn as a single strand, and a clasp may then be necessary.

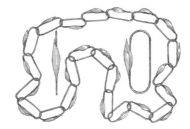
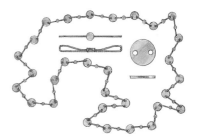

Fancy

Fancy need not mean complex, but intricate forms, details and textures can all add interest to a piece. If a necklace has a great deal of movement then stone settings or gloss finishes may be vulnerable.

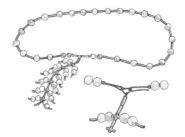
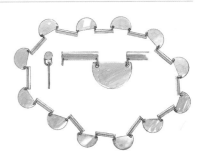

Pendants

On the chain

This method of hanging a pendant incorporates the chain as part of the form of the piece, either permanently, or as a removable part. Hanging a pendant in this way is a useful means of avoiding the use of a bale or loop fitting.

Centre pieces

A pendant is often the focal point of a neckpiece. A complex, eye-catching visual effect may be achieved by considering in combination the form, size, colour, texture and detail of the piece.

BROOCHES AND PINS

SIMPLE

A small decorative pin is often preferable to a larger brooch because it can be easily worn on the lapel or on lightweight fabrics. Pins can be inherently simple, and can project a sense of completion.

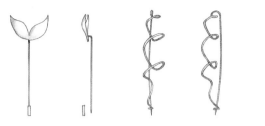

SINGLE PINS

The single-pinned brooch should be fastened so that the pin points from right to left. The opening mechanism of the clasp should point downwards, allowing gravity to help keep the pin from coming undone.

DOUBLE PINS

Double pins are better suited to large, heavy or long pieces than single pins. The double pin allows the piece to be positioned securely, keeping excess movement to a minimum. Although relatively easy to make, this is a more sophisticated form of pin.

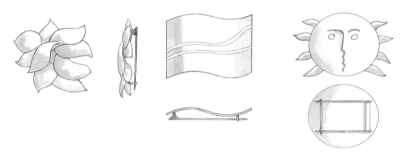

BANGLES AND WRIST PIECES

CUFF

A wrist piece with an open form can be worn without passing over the hand, thus avoiding any difficulties that may occur if the hand of the wearer is disproportionately larger than his or her wrist.

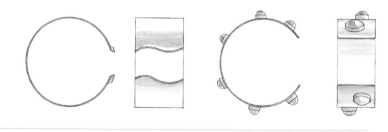

SIMPLE

The simple bangle that is clean in both form and design can be satisfying in its purity. Simple forms can often be surprisingly difficult to fabricate, because there are generally fewer details to mask blemishes.

BRACELETS

SIMPLE

With bracelets, visual simplicity tends to indicate technical simplicity. Fine linking detail should be avoided, as snagging is likely to occur, and finer bracelets could be damaged.

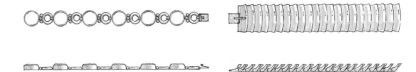

STONE SET

Stones can be used to add highlights, colour and visual impact to bracelets. Because of potential wear, stones require protection; this can be achieved in a variety of innovative ways, including the addition of granulation or detail round the edge of the stone.

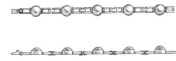

CUFFLINKS

SIMPLE

Simple cufflinks may be defined as those that are easily made using simple forms. A simple form can be dressed up using a variety of techniques, such as mill-pressing, to add texture, and patination, to add colour.

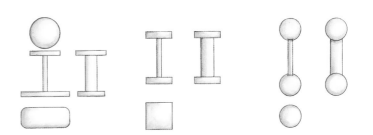

DOUBLE FACED

The double-faced cufflink allows for greater variety and interest than the traditional single-faced version, as the two faces need not have the same detail or form. One of the faces must, however, be able to pass through a buttonhole.

CHAIN LINKED

Chain-linked cufflinks have great physical flexibility, although they can be difficult to handle as a result. The chain must be strong enough to withstand the stress of any accidental wrenching.

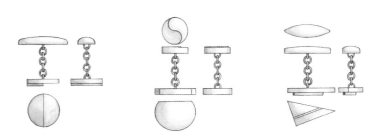

DIRECTORY OF GEMS

Choosing stones is fun, but making sure that you pick suitable stones can be tricky. Beginners should use larger, oval or round stones called cabochons because it is easier to make settings for them. Choose stones that have flat, even bottoms and that seem to be clear and bright. Check for chips or faults. Do not buy a stone with a lengthwise fault because it can split easily.

BEGINNER STONES

The stones listed below are a few of the most popular and easy-to-use stones for the beginner.

AMETHYST
Availability/price: Amethyst is a popular and affordable stone. A deep uniform purple colour is more expensive than the pale lavenders.
Colour: Amethyst can be found in all shades of purple, from light lavender (or rose) to the rich purple of Siberian amethyst, which displays magenta highlights when faceted. If the colour is too deep, the material can appear almost black.
Working with amethyst: Heat and strong sunlight can fade the material.

YELLOW QUARTZ (CITRINE)
Availability/price: Citrine is plentiful, available in large sizes and much less expensive than topaz. The darker the colour, the more expensive the material becomes. Heat-treated citrines are cheaper than natural material.
Colour: Citrine ranges from pastel lemon yellow to deep reddish brown and amber.
Working with citrine: Citrine is easily scratched and will change colour with prolonged exposure to strong light or heat.

SMOKY QUARTZ
Availability/price: Smoky quartz is plentiful and available in large sizes, making it extremely economical.
Colour: Smoky quartz appears in a range of subtle colours including yellowish brown, rich chocolate, charcoal brown and nearly black. Much of the material on the market has been colour enhanced or modified.
Working with smoky quartz: The material is easily scratched or chipped and will fade if exposed to intense heat or direct sunlight.

GARNET
Availability/price: Garnet costs slightly more than other gemstones of the same size and carat price. The dark red stone is low-priced and abundant; colour-change and mandarin garnets are extremely valuable; and rhodolite and spessartite garnets are mid-price.
Colour: Garnet includes almost every colour from blood red, violet-red and orange-red to green and yellow-brown.
Working with garnet: When setting faceted stones, take care to avoid chipping the girdle.

FLUORITE

Availability/price: Fluorite is an abundant and inexpensive material.

Colour: Fluorite comes in a variety of pretty transparent to translucent colours: golden yellow, bluish green, rose pink, blue, green, purple and colourless.

Working with fluorite: Its softness makes fluorite suitable for carving cameos and intaglios. It is a fragile material that cleaves and splits if heated or knocked. Store fluorite separately and wrap rows of beads individually. The intense colours can fade with extended exposure to sunlight.

PERIDOT

Availability/price: Peridot is readily available in paler colours, which are moderately priced. Larger, intensely coloured stones sell for high prices.

Colour: Peridot only ever comes in green – pale yellowish green, olive green, bottle green or apple green. The material is transparent but can contain inclusions.

Working with peridot: Peridot can be difficult to facet and polish, picks up scratches relatively easily, is quite sensitive to heat and is damaged by sulfuric and hydrochloric acids.

OPAL

Availability/price: The better and more even the colour, the higher the price.

Colour: The vibrant colours result from the diffraction of light off silica spheres inside the stone. This is called colour play or iridescence.

Working with opal: Opal is easily damaged by pressure and impact. Heat may cause cracking and a loss of colour play. Opal is sensitive to acids and alkalis and vulnerable to perfumes, soaps and detergents.

AMBER

Availability/price: Amber is a low-priced stone and the different colours have only minor variations in cost.

Colour: Yellow, golden brown, white, green, violet, red or black, amber varies from transparent to virtually opaque. It often contains insects and lichens.

Working with amber: Amber can be cut and carved with steel blades or abrasives, but is slightly brittle and tricky to drill. Cool during polishing to prevent damage. Acids, caustic solutions, gasoline and alcohol affect the lustre and heat causes cracks.

CUBIC ZIRCONIA

Availability/price: One of the best diamond simulants so far, cubic zirconia is widely available and inexpensive.

Colour: Cubic zirconia is usually colourless but may be made in a variety of colours.

Working with cubic zirconia: Unlike diamond, cubic zirconia can be scratched with a fine carbide scriber. Cubic zirconia retains its sparkle and polishes well. Do not let it rub against other gemstones, particularly diamond, because this will cause wear and scratching.

TOPAZ

Availability/price:
Topaz is generally good value for money.

Colour: Topaz ranges from yellow, yellow-brown, orange-brown and pink-brown to red, blue and colourless. Heat-treated topaz provides more intense colours.

Working with topaz:
Topaz is impervious to most scratching, but a slight blow along the stone's length could cause it to divide, so take care during setting. Brown-yellow topaz may lose colour when exposed to direct sunlight or too much heat.

MOONSTONE

Availability/price: Comes in large sizes and is good value for money. Rainbow is the cheapest and blue is the most expensive.

Colour: Moonstone can be transparent with a blue surface schiller; translucent or milky; or with a cat's-eye or star effect. It comes in a range of colours and inclusions are common.

Working with moonstone:
A slight blow, or too much pressure, will break a stone in two, so take care when setting, soldering and polishing jewellery.

CARNELIAN (ALSO CALLED CORNELIAN)

Availability/price: With the exception of the best red-orange material, carnelian is relatively inexpensive and readily available.

Colour: Carnelian ranges from a pure, intense red-orange to softer brownish oranges and reds. High-quality material is semitransparent and the colour seems to glow. The colour of carnelian can be enhanced by heating and dyeing. Natural carnelian has no banding or colour zoning.

Working with carnelian:
No special care is needed.

ONYX

Availability/price: Onyx is readily available and generally affordable, although good-quality material can sell for high prices.

Colour: In its natural state, onyx has straight bands of white and earthy brown colours. Black onyx is not onyx but dyed black agate or chalcedony.

Working with onyx: Onyx is popular for cameo and carving work because of its layered structure. To prevent chips or cracking, protect onyx from scratches and knocks and store it carefully.

Buying from a shop or dealer

Recent advances in gem treatments and synthetic stones have made buying gemstones much more of a challenge. It is crucial to see the stone in person and to find a supplier you can trust. Do your homework first. If you research prices it will help you judge whether a supplier is overcharging. Get to know which gemstones are most frequently treated. If you are buying a valuable gem, ask a laboratory to do a grading report on colour treatment. Check the credentials of the supplier and find out how long they have been in business. Make sure that the supplier has a fair and clear returns policy. A reputable supplier will guarantee merchandise by stating exactly what the goods are on a receipt and will always agree to a lab report.

When you visit a shop or dealer you will be faced by a bewildering number of stones, each varying in quality and price. It is easy to feel overwhelmed and to forget to look at the stones in detail. Never buy a stone without handling it first, but ask before you take it out of the box. The most important characteristics of a stone are hardness and colour. Depending on the stone, you should also consider optical effects, clarity, inclusions, durability, cut and treatment, if any.

Buying on the Internet

The Federal Trade Commission (FTC) has reported that information given in support of online gem sales is frequently inaccurate, incomplete or unreliable. The goods tend to be overpriced and sometimes are never delivered. Internet sales can lock you into a deal before you have had the chance to see or compare the gems firsthand.

Buying at trade events

Trade shows tend to be noisy, short of space, packed with people and have appalling lighting – all of which make it very difficult to assess a stone accurately. Traders often return overseas after the event, making it difficult to return faulty or misrepresented goods. To get a good deal, you'll need to be fast and accurate at assessing a stone and be able to stand your ground with some very persuasive dealers.

Useful information

When you are using metals and solders to make jewellery it is useful to know their basic properties.

Properties of gold

Fine or pure gold, 24 carat, is very soft and needs to be alloyed with other metals before it is hard enough to use. Like all precious metals, gold should be annealed before it is worked (see page 48). Higher carat golds stay softer for longer than those below 14 carat because of their higher gold content. Metal will only harden as it is worked, so if annealed gold is left for several days, it will not have hardened by the time you resume work on it. 18 carat gold contains 18 parts in 24 of fine gold, 9 carat gold contains 9 parts in 24 of fine gold and so on.

Properties of silver

Sterling silver contains 925 parts in 1000 of fine silver – a small amount of copper is added to pure silver to make a more durable metal. It is easy to use but is not as strong as gold. During heating, black copper oxides penetrate the surface creating 'fire stain', a black stain, which has to be removed. Silver is a malleable metal but will work-harden after a while. It is annealed to keep it soft and workable.

Properties of brass and copper

Both of these metals are easy to use, especially for beginners as they are inexpensive, but they do not retain a polished surface and are quickly work-hardened.

Melting temperatures of commonly used metals in jewellery making

Metal	*Melting point °C	*Melting point °F
Aluminium	660	1,220
Brass	935	1,715
Copper	1,083	1,981
Gold 24 carat	1,063	1,945
Gold 22 carat	980	1,796
Gold 18 carat	960	1,760
Gold 14 carat	870	1,598
Gold 9 carat	900	1,652
Nickel	1,455	2,651
Silver fine	961	1,762
Silver sterling	920	1,688
Platinum	1,745	3,173
Steel	1,430	2,606
Steel stainless	1,450	2,642
Titanium	1,800	3,272

*Melting points are approximate

Conversion charts

Metal thicknessess
Precise metric and imperial gauge conversions

mm	B&S gauge	inches		mm	B&S gauge	inches
6.54	2	0.258		0.81	20	0.032
5.19	4	0.204		0.64	22	0.025
4.11	6	0.162		0.51	24	0.020
3.26	8	0.129		0.40	26	0.015
2.59	10	0.102		0.33	28	0.013
2.05	12	0.081		0.25	30	0.010
1.63	14	0.064		0.20	32	0.008
1.29	16	0.051		0.16	34	0.006
1.02	18	0.040		0.13	36	0.005

Ring sizes

UK	US	EU	mm	inches	UK	US	EU	mm	inches
A	½		37.83	1.490	N	6 ¾		53.47	2.107
A ½	¾		38.42	1.514	N ½	14		54.10	2.132
B	1		39.02	1.537	O	7	15	54.74	2.157
B ½	1 ¼		39.62	1.561	O ½	7 ¼		55.38	2.182
C	1 ½		40.22	1.585	P	7 ½	16	56.02	2.207
C ½	1 ¾		40.82	1.608	P ½	7 ¾		56.66	2.232
D	2	1	41.42	1.632	Q	8	17	57.30	2.257
D ½	2 ¼	2	42.02	1.655	Q ½	8 ¼	18	57.94	2.283
E	2 ½		42.61	1.679	R	8 ½		58.57	2.308
E ½	2 ¾	3	43.21	1.703	R ½	8 ¾	19	59.21	2.333
F	3	4	43.81	1.726	S	9	20	59.85	2.358
F ½			44.41	1.750	S ½	9 ¼		60.49	2.383
G	3 ¼	5	45.01	1.773	T	9 ½	21	61.13	2.408
G ½	3 ½		45.61	1.797	T ½	9 ¾	22	61.77	2.434
H	3 ¾	6	46.20	1.820	U	10		62.40	2.459
H ½	4		46.80	1.844	U ½	10 ¼	23	63.04	2.484
I	4 ¼	7	47.40	1.868	V	10 ½	24	63.68	2.509
I ½	4 ½	8	48.00	1.891	V ½	10 ¾		64.32	2.534
J	4 ¾		48.60	1.915	W	11	25	64.88	2.556
J ½	5	9	49.20	1.938	W ½	11 ¼		65.48	2.580
K	5 ¼	10	49.80	1.962	X	11 ½	26	66.07	2.603
K ½	5 ½		50.39	1.986	X ½	11 ¾		66.67	2.627
L	5 ¾	11	50.99	2.009	Y	12		67.27	2.650
L ½	6		51.59	2.033	Y ½	12 ¼		67.87	2.674
M	6 ¼	12	52.19	2.056	Z	12 ½		68.47	2.680
M ½	6 ½	13	52.79	2.080					

GLOSSARY

Abrasives
The natural or man-made sand-like particles used to smooth or clean away marks on a surface, as can be found adhered to emery papers.

Adhesive
Sticky substance, such as glue, used for sticking things together.

Alloy
A mixture of metals.

Aluminium
A lightweight, light grey, malleable ductile metal.

Ball pein hammer
Hammer with one flat end and one ball end used for shaping and texturing metal.

Base metal
Nonprecious metal such as aluminium, brass, copper, gilding metal, nickel, pewter, steel and titanium.

Bevel
Slant or inclination.

Bezel
The rim of metal that is used to secure a stone in rub-over setting.

Binding wire
Steel wire used to secure components together during soldering.

Borax
Flux, used to prevent fire stain when soldering.

Brass
A metal similar to copper but slightly coarser and lighter in colour.

Bronze
A pale yellow metal used for casting that is generally an alloy of copper and tin.

Burr
Metal tools for grinding, for use with a pendant motor or a hobby drill.

Burnish
To polish by rubbing.

Cabochon
An uncut, polished stone.

Calipers
A tool used for the measurement of sheet, wire and holes.

Calotte
Used to cover knots on strung necklaces.

Carat
A measure used to express the purity of gold with 24 being the purest.

Clasp
A means of securing a bracelet, neckpiece or other piece of jewellery.

Charcoal block
Used in soldering, reflects heat well.

Claw
The name given to describe a prong used to set a stone in claw a setting.

Compound
Also polishing compound. Generic name for a greasy media containing abrasives used in the polishing process.

Cones and end caps
These are used to finish multistranded necklaces and bracelets.

Copper
A reddish-coloured, malleable metal.

Countersink
The enlargement of the entry to a hole.

Crimp
Metal tube used to secure beads onto the ends of beaded jewellery. The crimp is flattened so it grips the strands.

Crimp cover
A decorative cover for a crimp.

Cutting list
The list of materials that is made with dimensions and quantities to facilitate ordering.

Doming block
A steel form with hemispherical depressions used to form domes.

Doming punches
Steel punches with rounded heads used with a doming block to make domes.

Faceted
A term used to describe gemstones that have been cut so that their form is covered in small, polished, flat surfaces.

Ferrous
Containing iron.

Fibre grips
Protective covering used to protect material from being damaged by the steel jaws of a vice.

Fibula
A brooch where the pin is integral to the form, similar to a safety pin.

Findings
A term used to describe the commercially-made fittings for jewellery purposes.

Finish
A term used to describe the cleaning up of a piece by sanding and polishing.

Fire stain
Also fire scale.
A layer of subcutaneous discolouration on sterling/standard silver that is the result of annealing or soldering.

Flat steel plate
Hard steel plate used in forging.

Flux
The generic term used to describe a chemical used as an antioxidant as part of the soldering process.

Former
A form, generally made of steel, used to support metal while it is being formed.

Fretwork
A term used to describe a sheet that has been pierced with a number of holes to make an ornamental pattern.

Gauge
A standard of measurement such as the thickness of sheet or the diameter of wire.

Gimp
Tube made of coiled fine wire used to protect threads in stringing.

Gold
The metal most commonly associated with jewellery, it is naturally found as a rich yellow colour although it can be alloyed to be white, red or green in colour.

Hammer
A tool for beating or striking metal.

Heat-resistant tweezers
Tweezers used in soldering and annealing for holding metal while it is very hot.

Imperial
Non-metric standard of measure or weight.

Join
A term used to describe the meeting of two or more pieces for soldering.

Joint
Another term used to describe join.

Jump ring
Generic word for plain ring forms used in jewellery, not including finger rings.

Malleable
A term used to describe a material that can be readily formed, rolled, etc.

Mallet
Non-metal-faced hammer.

Mandrel
Another name for a former.

Metric
Relating to measurement based on the decimal system.

Mop
Also buffing wheel.
Fabric polishing end.

Nickel
A pale silvery metal also known as nickel silver.

Non-ferrous
Metals not containing iron.

Pallions
Also chips.
Term for pieces of solder, taken from the French word 'flake'.

Patina
A surface finish that develops on metal or other material as a result of exposure to chemicals or handling.

Pickle
A chemical used to remove the oxides that are a result of heating.

Piercing saw
A saw with a narrow blade that can be threaded though a drill hole.

Pin
A piece of wire with a sharpened end used to fasten an object.

Planishing
Polishing or flattening by hammering with a mirror-finished hammer face.

Platinum
Grey precious metal.

Precious

A term used to describe diamonds, sapphires, rubies and emeralds when referring to stones or gold, silver and platinum when referring to metals.

Punches

Hardened steel tools used in forming or texturing metal.

Pusher

A tool used in stone setting to push metal over the stone.

Quench

Cooling hot metal in water after annealing or soldering.

Reticulation

A method of heating metal to cause a surface texture.

Rivets

A bolt used to join two or more pieces.

Rods

Straight solid wire.

Rub-over setting

A type of stone setting that uses a bezel.

Rolling mill

Equipment used for decreasing the thickness of metal and for applying textures.

Rouge

Polishing compound used for the final stages of polishing.

Scribe

A sharp metal implement used for marking designs onto metal.

Shank

Straight or plain section of a ring or twist drill bit.

Sheet

A piece of metal that is normally of uniform thickness.

Silver

A light grey metal that is malleable and ductile.

Solder

A fusible alloy for joining metals.

Sprung tweezers

Self-locking tweezers or fibre grip tweezers that close when you release them. Used as a soldering aid.

Steel

A grey ferrous metal often used for tool making.

Table

The top face of a faceted stone.

Template

A shaped, thin plate used as a guide to define a form.

Thrumming

Polishing with threads.

Toggle

A bar or other form used to fasten and prevent slipping through a hole.

Triblet

Another term for a mandrel or former.

Tripoli

Polishing compound used in the first stages of polishing.

Vernier

A sliding scale used for accurate fractional measurement.

Work-hardening

The hardening of a material by manipulation.

FURTHER READING

MAGAZINES

Crafts
44a Pentonville Road
London N1 9BY
United Kingdom
Tel: +44 (0) 20 7806 2542
www.craftscouncil.org.uk

Retail Jeweller
33–39 Bowling Green Lane
London EC1R 0DA
United Kingdom
Tel: +44 (0) 20 7812 3724
www.retail-jeweller.com

Lapidary Journal Jewelry Artist
The trusted guide to the art of gems, jewellery making, design, beads, minerals and more.
300 Chesterfield Parkway
Suite 100
Malvern, Pennsylvania 19355
Tel: 610-232-5700
www.jewelryartistmagazine.com

Metalsmith
Society of North American Goldsmiths
540 Oak Street, Suite A
Eugene, Oregon 97401
Tel: 541-345-5689
www.snagmetalsmith.org

Colored Stone
An international trade magazine covering all aspects of the gemstone industry.
300 Chesterfield Parkway
Suite 100
Malvern, Pennsylvania 19355
Tel: 610-232-5700
www.colored-stone.com

Step by Step Wire Jewelry
The magazine for wire jewellery makers of all levels.
300 Chesterfield Parkway
Suite 100
Malvern, Pennsylvania 19355
Tel: 610-232-5700
www.stepbystepwire.com

BOOKS

Jeweller's Directory of Gemstones
Crowe, Judith
A&C Black, 2006

Britain's Best Museums and Galleries
Fisher, Mark
Allen Lane, 2004

The Art of Metal Clay
Haab, Sherri
Roundhouse Publishing Group, 2007

Jewellery: Fundamentals of Metalsmithing
McCreight, Tim
A&C Black, 1998

Complete Metalsmith
McCreight, Tim
Davis Publications, 2004

The Jeweller's Directory of Shape and Form
Olver, Elizabeth
A&C Black, 2001

The Art of Jewellery Design
Olver, Elizabeth
A&C Black, 2002

Jewelry Concepts and Technology
Untracht, Oppi
Doubleday, 1982

Ethnic Jewellery
Van de star, Renee
Pepin Press, 2006

WEBSITES

www.jewelrymaking.about.com
www.snagmetalsmiths.org
www.whoswhoingoldandsilver.com
www.jaa.co.au
www.acj.org.uk

INDEX

Page numbers in bold type are
for glossary references

a

abrasives **122**
accident prevention 9
adhesive **122**
alloy **122**
aluminum **122**
amber 117
amethyst 116
annealing 48–49
Archimedian drill 15, 34

b

bale 88–89
ball pein hammer 14, **122**
bangles
  design ideas for 114
  textured 73–74
base metal **122**
bead board 108
beads 76–78, 100–109
bench vice 15
bending, wire 50–51, 54,
  64–65
bending tools 13, 64–65
bevel **122**
bezel **122**
bezel wire 90
binding wire 16, **122**
books, as source of ideas 21
borax cone and dish 16
borax (flux) 38, **122**
bracelets
  design ideas for 115
  domed 79–81
  link bracelet 96–99
brass 120, **122**
brass sheet 17
bronze **122**
brooches
  design ideas for 114
  fretwork brooch 62–63
  pierced brooch 33
  stone-set brooch 33
brush, for flux 16, 38
burnish/burnishing 45, **122**
burnisher 17, 45
burr **122**

buying materials 27
  gemstones 119

c

cabochon **122**
calipers **122**
calottes 102–103, **123**
carat **122**
carnelian (cornelian) 118
centre punch 15
chain necklace 52–53
chains
  polishing 44
  soldering 40
charcoal block **122**
clamps 15
clasp **122**
claw **122**
colour, and temperature 41, 48
compounds, polishing 17, 43, **122**
cones **122**
copper 120, **122**
copper sheet 17
countersink **122**
crimp covers 102, **122**
crimps and crimping 101, **122**
cubic zirconia 117
cufflinks
  design ideas for 115
  riveted 84–85
curves
  bending wire into 50
  filing techniques 37
  forging techniques 58
cutting tools 13

d

D-shaped silver wire 17
design ideas 20–23, 112–115
  planning a design 24–27
dividers 12
dome bracelet 79–81
domed beads 76–78
doming block 14, 75, **122**
doming punches 14, 75, **122**
doming techniques 75–78
drawing design plans 24
  on metal 25
drilling techniques 34–35
drilling tools 15, 34–35

e

earring posts 87
earring wires 87–88
earrings
  design ideas for 112
  textured 70–72
emery papers and boards 17, 42
emery stick 42
end cutters 13
exhibitions 21

f

faceted **122**
ferrous **122**
fibre grips **122**
fibula **123**
files 12, 36
filing techniques 36–37
findings 86–89, **123**
finish **123**
finishing techniques 42–45, 61
fire stain **123**
flat steel plate 14, 59, **123**
fluorite 117
flux (borax) 38, **123**
forged ring 60–61
forging techniques 58–61
former **123**
forming tools 14
fretwork **123**
fretwork brooch 62–63

g

galleries, as source of ideas 21
garnet 116
gauge **123**
gemstones 90, 105, 116–119
gimp **123**
gold 120, **123**

h

hammering techniques
  forging 58–59
  texturing 66
hammers 14, 59, **123**
hand drill 35
health and safety 9, 41, 44,
  66
heat-resistant tweezers 16, 40,
  123

hobby drill kit 45
hollow domed beads 76–78

i

ideas file 20, 22, 112–115
imperial **123**
inspiration, and design 20–23
inspiration exercise 23
Internet
  buying gemstones on 119
  as source of ideas 21

j

join **123**
jump rings 51, 86–87, **123**

k

knotting techniques 100

l

link bracelet 96–99
loops, wire 103–105

m

magazines, as source of ideas 21
malleable **123**
mallets 14, **123**
mandrel 14, **123**
marking tools 12
materials 17, 27
  see also brass; copper;
    gemstones; gold; metal;
    platinum; silver; wire
measuring tools 12
melting temperatures 120
metal
  annealing 48–49, 58
  fixing pattern onto 26–27
  forging 58–59
  thicknesses 121
  transferring design to 25
metal sheet 17, 27
metric **123**
moonstone 118
mops 45, **122**
multistrand necklace 108–109
museums, as source of ideas 21

n

natural objects 21
necklaces
  design ideas for 113
  multistrand 108–109
  simple chain 52–53
  strung beads 106–107
needle files 12, 36, 37
nickel **123**
non-ferrous **123**

o

onyx 118
opal 117

p

pallions **123**
patina **123**
pendant motor 15, 45, 67
pendants
  design ideas for 113
  with rub-over setting 94–95
  simple silver 46–47
  twisted wire 57
peridot 117
pickle/pickling 41, **123**
pierced brooch 33
piercing saw 13, 30, **123**
piercing techniques 30–33
piercing tools 13, 30–31
pin **123**
pin hammer 14
planishing **123**
planishing hammer 14
platinum **124**
pliers 13
polishing compounds 17, 43, **122**
polishing motor 43
polishing techniques 42–45
polishing tools 17, 42–43
power drill 34–35
precious **124**
punches 14, 15, **122**, **124**
pusher 17, **124**

q

quench **124**

r

raising hammer 14
rawhide (wooden) mallet 14
reticulation 67, **124**
right angle, bending wire into 65
ring clamp 15
ring mandrel (bangle mandrel) 14
ring sizes 121
rings
  bezel-set 93
  design ideas for 112
  forged ring 60–61
  for simple chain necklace 52–53
  simple silver ring 54–55
rink shank, filing 37
riveted cufflinks 84–85
riveting techniques 82–83
rivets **124**
rods **124**
rolling mill 68, **124**
rouge **124**
round silver wire 17
rub-over setting 90–95, **124**

s

safety precautions 9, 41, 44, 66
saw blades 13, 31
scribe 12, **124**
semi-precious gems 90, 105, 116–119
setting, rub-over 90–95
shank 37, **124**
shapes
  ideas for 112–115
  as source of ideas 21
  three-dimensional 75–76
  wire shapes 51
shaping tools 12
sheet metal 17, 27, **124**
silver 120, **124**
silver sheet 17
silver solder 16
silver wire 17
sketchbooks 20, 22
smoky quartz 116
smoothing techniques 42
smoothing tools 12
snips 13

solder 16, 38, 39, **124**
soldering brick 16
soldering equipment 16, 38
soldering techniques 38–41
soldering torch 16
spiral, wire 51
sprung tweezers **124**
steel **124**
steel ruler 12
stone-set brooch 33
stones
  rub-over setting 90–93
  semi-precious 90, 105, 116–119
strung necklace 106–107

t

table **124**
temperature, and colour 41, 48
temperature, melting 120
template **124**
textured bangle 73–74
textured earrings 70–72
texturing techniques 52, 66–69
thrumming **124**
toggle **124**
tools 12–17
  using 30–31, 34–35, 42–43, 64–65, 68
topaz 118
trade events 119
triblet **124**
tripoli **124**
tweezers 16, 40, **124**
twisting wire 56–57

v

vernier **124**
vices 15

w

wire
  bending techniques 50–51, 54, 64–65
  forging techniques 60–61
  for rub-over setting 90–92
  silver 17
  twisting techniques 56–57
wire loops 103–105
wire shapes 51

workbench 19
work-hardening **124**
working drawings 24
workspace 18–19
wrapped loop 104–105
wrist pieces see bangles; bracelets

y

yellow quartz (citrine) 116

CREDITS

Quarto would like to thank the following for kindly supplying images for inclusion in this book:

Key: a = above, b = below, c = centre,
l = left, r = right

p.23acl Lebedev Maksim/Shutterstock
p.23al Jasenka Luksa/Shutterstock
p.23br Timothy Craig Lubcke/Shutterstock
p.23c Ivan Cholakov/Shutterstock
p.23cl Lagui/Shutterstock
p.33b Madeleine Coles
p.33c Elizabeth Olver
p.78b Shelby Fitzpatrick (photographer Mike Blissett)
p.89 bc John Field
p.89br Rauni Higson
p.105bl Charmian Harris
p.105br Guen Palmer
p.117b PjrFoto/studio/Alamy
p.118ar Arco Images/Alamy

All other images are the copyright of Quarto Publishing plc. While every effort has been made to credit contributors, Quarto would like to apologise should there have been any omissions or errors – and would be pleased to make the appropriate correction for future editions of the book.